AF822123

Praise for *How Hacks Happen and how to protect yourself*

"***How Hacks Happen*** is an eye-opening look at well, exactly how computer hacks happen! Although I work in social media, and I am on my computer most of the day, security is not always top of mind for me. I will readily admit to committing some of the security issues described in the book, and will be tightening up my passwords and watching more closely for phishing emails. If you have become a bit lackadaisical about your computer security, this book will set you on the path to a more secure future with easy to understand illustrations and instructions."

Corey Walker, author, ***Instagram for Dummies*** and ***Instagram for Dummies for Business***

"After working in Information Technology for the last 25 years, I have seen the growth in sophistication with hacking. Even people that are vigilant can be susceptible to hackers. The question is not if I get hacked, it is when I get hacked.

Mark does a great job of covering the current landscape of hacks and what you can do to try to protect yourself and your company. I especially like the exercises he includes on the topics. Do yourself a favor and go through each exercise. No really, do each exercise. It certainly opened my eyes to ideas I had not thought."

Chuck Moehling, Senior business analyst

"Mark's Book is great, easy to read, and a MUST for anyone who uses that thing called "THE WEB" and its related e-mail! I've been a business lawyer for over 30 years, believe I'm fairly knowledgeable about day-to-day operation of my computer and the internet, and (having been raised in a small-town by Depression-Era parents) have a healthy suspicious mind! Nonetheless, I fell for one of these "hacks" (the GOOGLE LOG-IN scam), about two years ago. Mark navigated me through "fixing it" after-the-fact, and WISH I'd read his book BEFORE!"

Franklin T. Watson, Attorney at Law

How Hacks Happen

and how to protect yourself

I did not appreciate my teachers at John Hersey High School enough. I did not appreciate my professors at Michigan State University enough.

That is, until I started writing books.

Mark Anthony Germanos

April 25, 2020

How Hacks Happen

and how to protect yourself

Cyber Safety Net
3450 Palmer Drive #4-286
Cameron Park, CA 95682 USA
mark@cybersafetynet.net
(844) 580-1200

Print ISBN: 978-0-9835769-2-1
E-book ISBN: 978-0-9835769-3-8
Library of Congress Control Number: 2020906116

Mark Anthony Germanos is not a lawyer. You are an adult. You are responsible for anything you do. Some names have been changed to protect those who make bad decisions. Everything from this point onward is the author's opinion.

Written by Mark Anthony Germanos
Edited by Holly Phillips
Designed by Holly Wolfe

How Hacks Happen

and how to protect yourself

Introduction

Somebody hacks you online. You click a link you should not have clicked. You look at the resulting web page without asking if it is legitimate. You type personal information and click OK. You inadvertently provide valuable information to a hacker. Maybe you have already experienced this.

You find out after-the-fact. Here are the symptoms:

1. You find unauthorized charges on your credit card bill.
2. A bank account has been drained to zero or your balance is unexplainably low.
3. You cannot access your files or your computer in general because all your files are encrypted, and someone is demanding a ransom payment.
4. You receive letters from your bank because your checks are being returned as Insufficient Funds. Yes, you're bouncing checks.
5. You apply for a loan and learn that someone in another city used your credit to purchase a big-ticket item, such as a car, while leveraging your credit score.
6. You receive notice from your insurer that someone — not you — has redeemed your benefits.
7. You receive an annual notice from the Social Security Administration advising you of your entitlements. They are lower than last year. You still work.

I am stopping at unlucky seven. Some of my industry's thought leaders feel getting exploited is a ***when*** question, not an ***if*** question. It is inevitable. Like getting in a car crash that is not your fault...it is inevitable.

My name is Mark Anthony Germanos and I know a thing or two about identity theft. A few years back, I opened my VISA statement and found a $1,000 charge on Christmas Day from a company I did not know. I protested the transaction and confirmed to my credit card issuer that I did not do the transaction. I was 100% sure it was fraudulent. They issued a chargeback.

I also promote myself as an ethical hacker. "What does that mean," you may ask. It means I use the skills and tactics hackers use to exploit their victims, but I have a different agenda. I find your vulnerabilities and help you remediate them ***before*** the bad guys find them. It's like asking the fire department to find ways a fire may start in your office ***before*** a fire happens.

I am writing with two personas. You may finish this book and feel two guys with different agendas wrote this. That is by design. Here are the personas:

Mark Anthony. As an ethical hacker, I look for vulnerabilities and help you remediate them. I advocate complex passwords because they are harder for hackers to crack. I advocate password managers because people like using the same password at multiple websites. If a thief learns a password you are using at one site, he will try that at others. I advocate protecting your digital assets, including your identity, with modern solutions. I believe security awareness training gives you the biggest bang for your buck and nullifies a hacker's easiest attack path into your systems. I believe everybody's security is too weak. If you are a client, you're probably rolling your eyes and saying "Yes Mark. We know. We know. We know..."

Brad Cracker. As a hacker, I know everybody has something valuable I can steal and sell. Bank account numbers. Credit card numbers. Social Security numbers. Medical record numbers. Passwords. I don't really care what you do or how much $$ you make. I just want something I can steal and sell. I am quite happy harvesting data and selling it in the form of a Microsoft Excel workbook on the dark web. What I do is ***not*** a crime. I channel my hacking activities through VPN connections. If your computer logs document my intrusion, they may report I was in Dubai, London or Reykjavik. Good luck finding me. I am in Sacramento.

Figure 1: Mark Anthony. The good guy. Wants to protect you

Figure 2: Brad Cracker. The bad guy. Wants to exploit you

Hats

What color hats do we wear?

The security industry labels hackers as white hack, black hat and grey hat. "How cute," you may say. Yes. They help explain hackers' mindsets. I am sharing content from https://blog.eccouncil.org/types-of-hackers-and-what-they-do-white-black-and-grey/.

Black hat hackers

'The term "black hat" originated from Western movies, where the bad guys wore black hats and the good guys wore white hats.

A black-hat hacker is an individual who attempts to gain unauthorized entry into a system or network to exploit them for malicious reasons. The black-hat hacker does not have any permission or authority to compromise their targets. They try to inflict damage by compromising security systems, altering functions of websites and networks, or shutting down systems. They often do so to steal or gain access to passwords, financial information, and other personal data.' Black hat hackers make headlines. Brad Cracker is a black hat hacker.

White hat hackers

'White-hat hackers, on the other hand, are deemed to be the good guys, working with organizations to strengthen the security of a system. A white hat has permission to engage the targets and to compromise them within the prescribed rules of engagement.

White-hat hackers are often referred to as ethical hackers. This individual specializes in ethical hacking tools, techniques, and methodologies to secure an organization's information systems. Unlike black-hat hackers, ethical hackers exploit security networks and look for backdoors when they are ***legally permitted*** to do so. White-hat hackers always disclose every vulnerability they find in the company's security system so that they can be fixed before they are being exploited by malicious actors. Some Fortune 50 companies like Facebook, Microsoft, and Google also use white-hat hackers.' Mark Anthony is a white hat hacker.

Grey hat hackers

'Grey hats exploit networks and computer systems in the way that black hats do, but do so without any malicious intent, disclosing all loopholes and vulnerabilities to law enforcement agencies or intelligence agencies.

Usually, grey-hat hackers surf the net and hack into computer systems to notify the administrator or the owner that their system/network contains one or more vulnerabilities that must be fixed immediately. Grey hats may also extort the hacked, offering to correct the defect for a nominal fee.'

Email Hack

This hack happens every day

Brad Cracker

You go to work. You arrive late, of course, because traffic moved slower than it should. You're frantic. You barely pay attention as you sit down at your desk and open your email.

You see one that warns your Gmail password will expire within 24 hours. '"Click here" to reset the password and acquire your email within 24 hours or your account will be exterminated' it says.

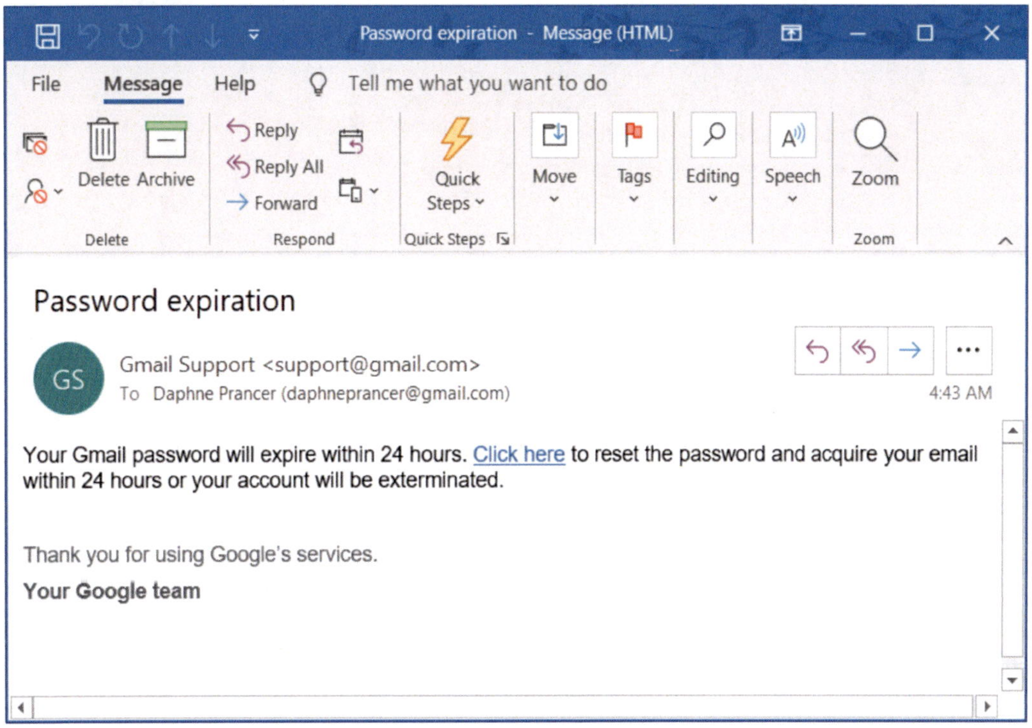

Figure 3: The first phish attack (fraudulent email) of the day

You click. Never mind that you have not had your morning coffee yet and you're still fuming about the slow commute.

"Gmail is my lifeblood," you mutter. "I better renew my account now because I cannot lose access." You type your email address, daphneprancer@gmail.com and click **Next**. The trick is on you. It only ***looks*** like Gmail.

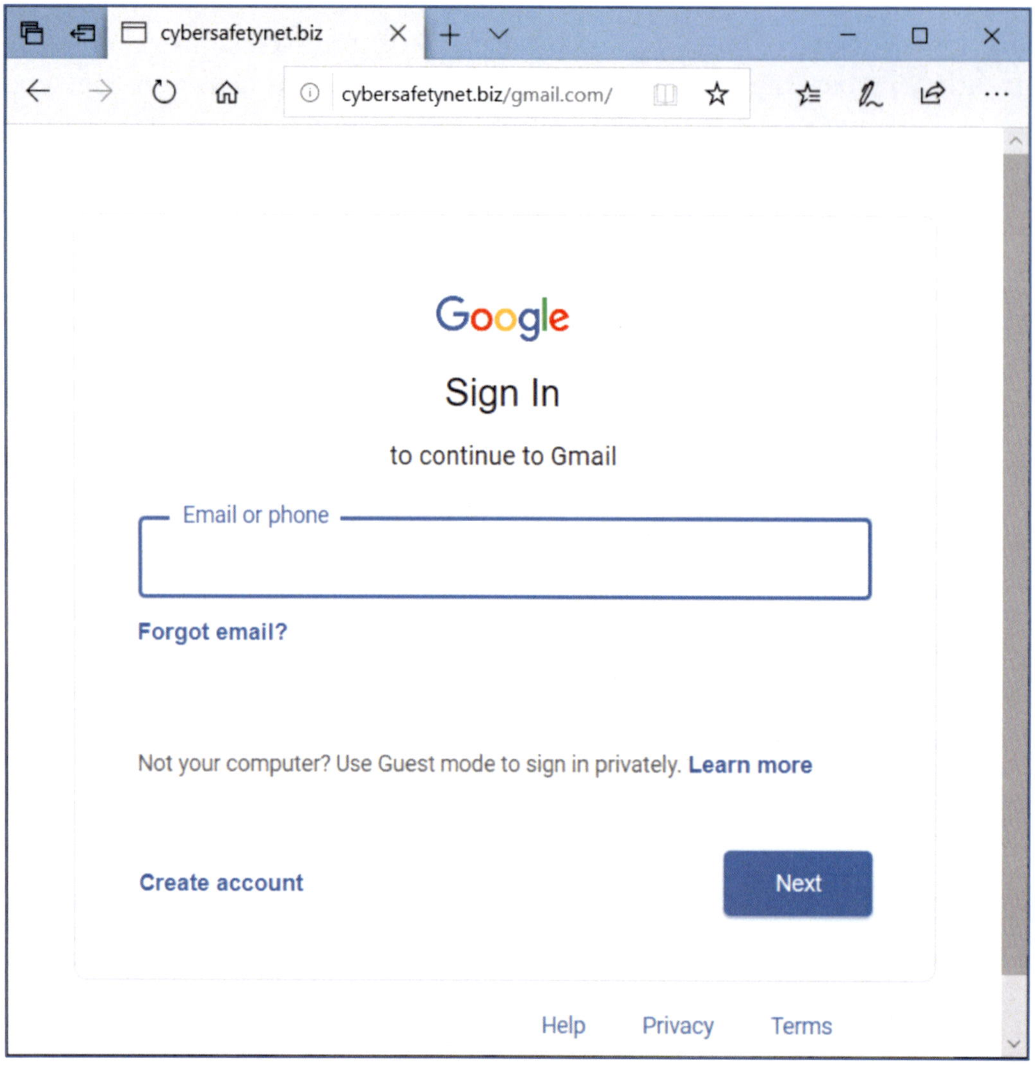

Figure 4: Type your Gmail address here

You type your password and click **Next**.

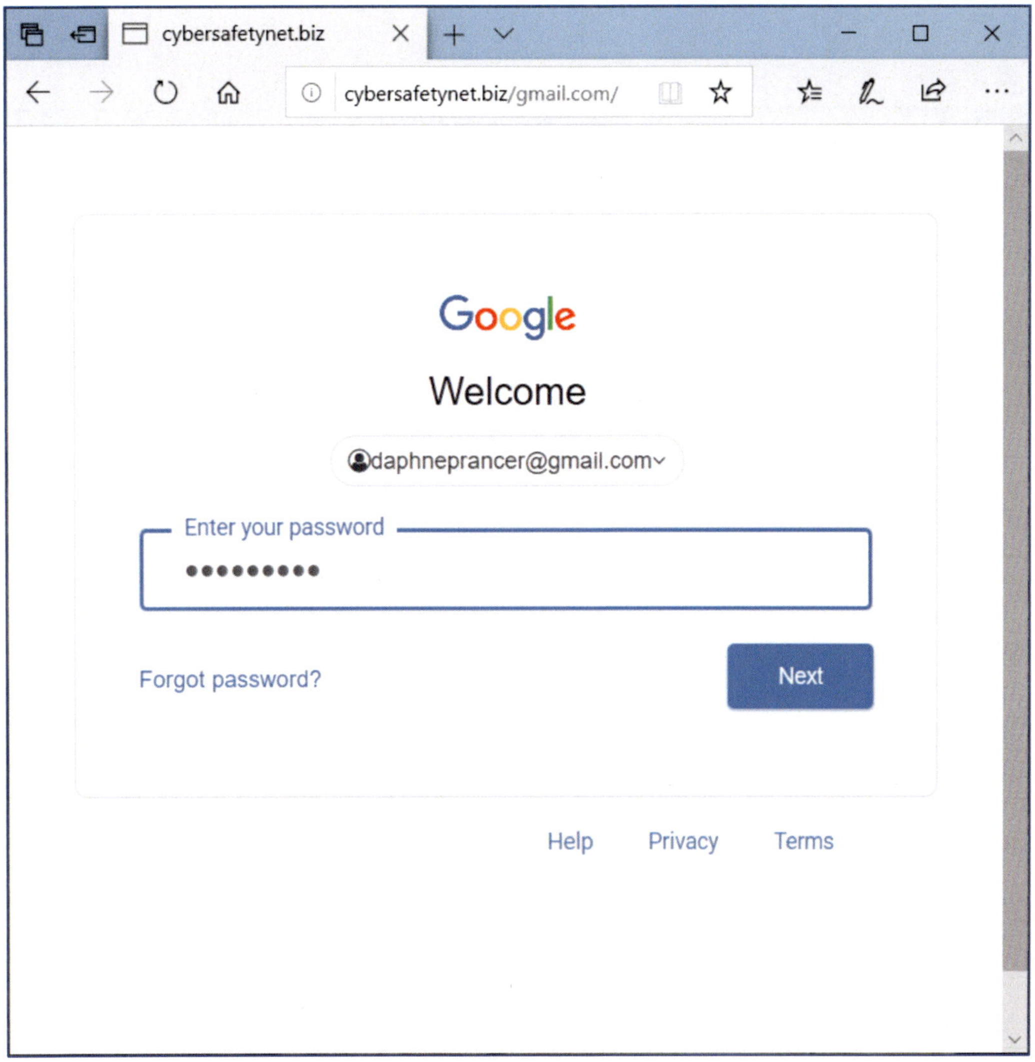

Figure 5: Think twice before you type your password

"Hmm," you say. "I typed my password right. Let me try again. My password is ***2018Prius***, right?" You successfully login to your Gmail account and go about your day.

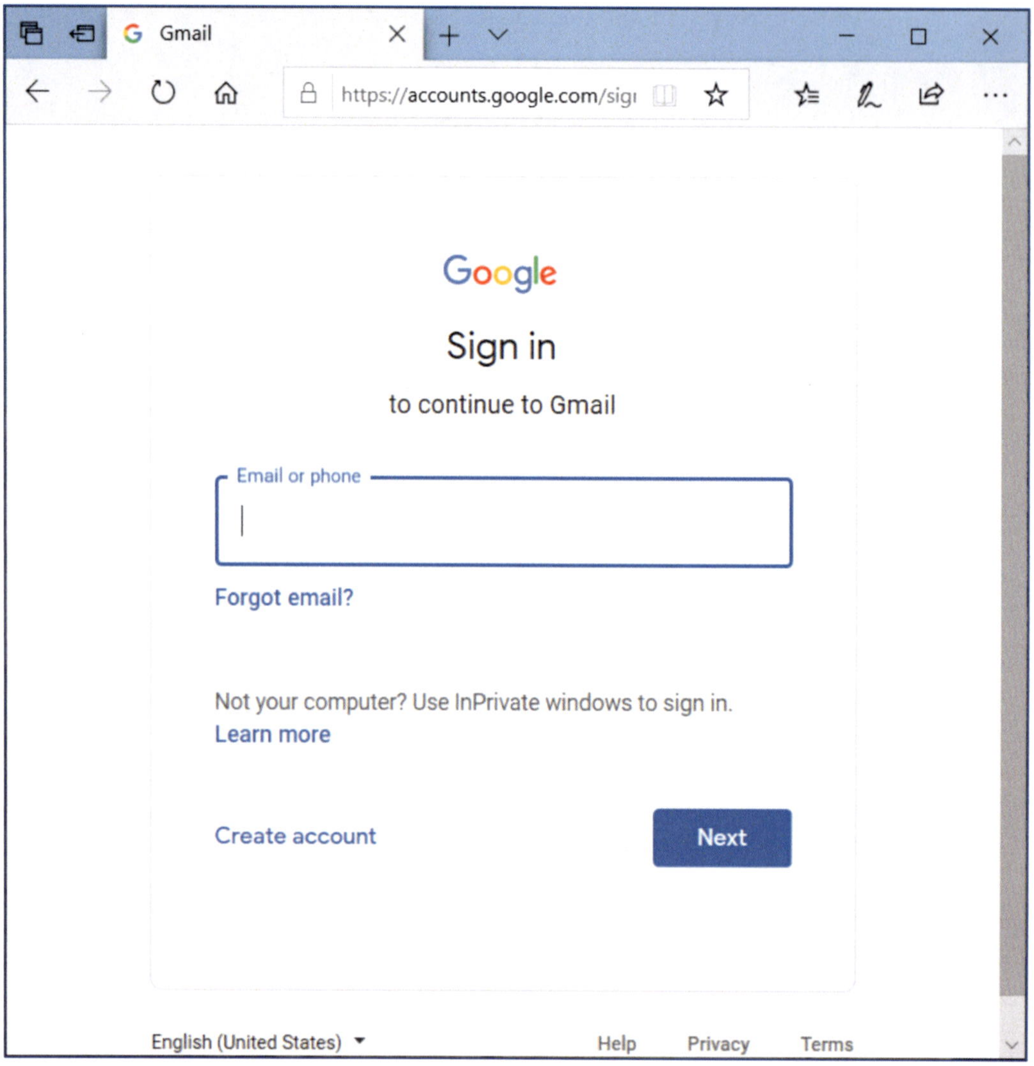

Figure 6: The real Gmail login page

You were right when you said, "My password is ***2018Prius***, right?" I know. You sent me an email.

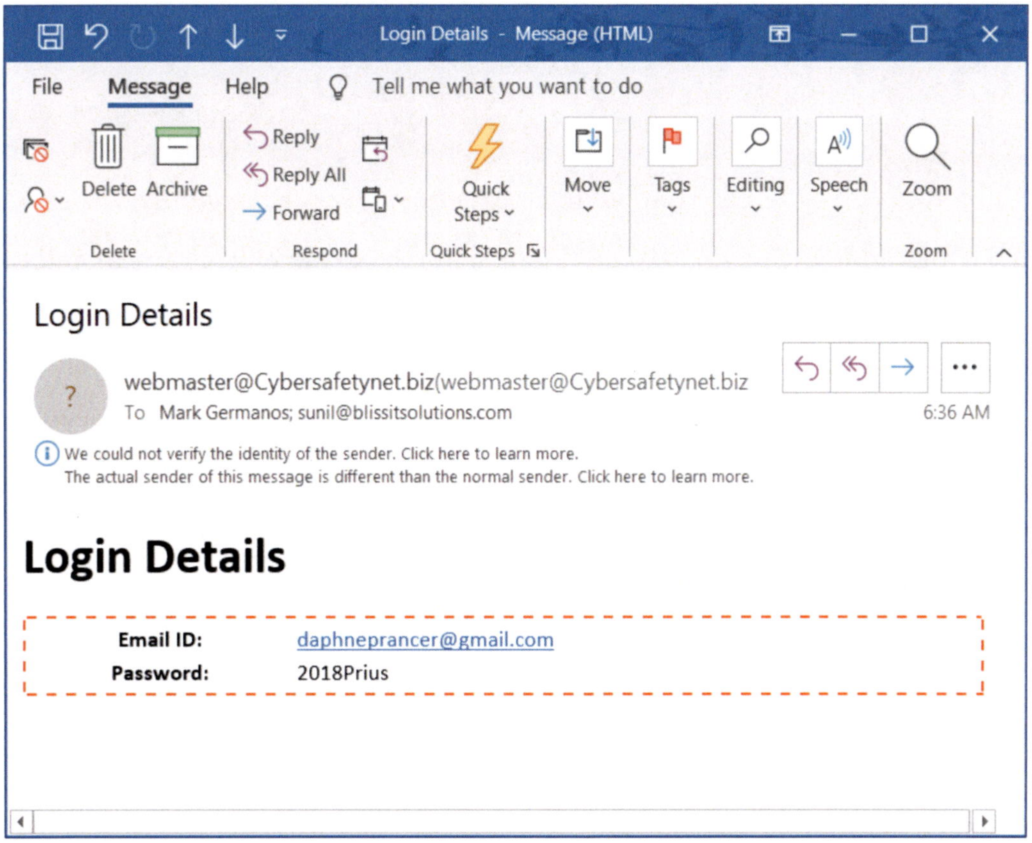

Figure 7: You fell into the trap and submitted your email and password

With this information, I can now login to your Gmail. I also bet that you use this same email and password at several different sites. Like most Americans, you feel you have too many passwords. You minimize the password burden by using the same password at various websites. Am I right? Yes. You know I am.

How this hack worked

1. I sent you a link. This one happened to appear in an email. I can send spam, create pop-ups or buy ads that entice you to click them without fully vetting the link (finding out where you would go if you do click the link).
2. I created the fake Gmail login page at http://cybersafetynet.biz/gmail.com. We call this a spoof, which https://en.wikipedia.org/wiki/Spoofed_URL reports is a website that poses as another website. You entered your email address on the spoof. Any email address would have worked here: did not have to be a Gmail address.
3. I created the fake password prompt. Any password you enter here will not work. Remember, you're at http://cybersafetynet.biz/gmail.com.

4. After you enter your password and press Next, my code redirects to the legitimate Gmail login page. You successfully enter your Gmail address and then on the next page, you enter your password and voila! You're in Gmail. You go about your day.
5. I read my email. One is from my website autoresponder. It presents the email address and password you provided.

Mark Anthony

This could have been avoided. That email Brad sent you was suspicious.

1. The link did not take you to Gmail. You could have hovered over the link to reveal the true destination, http://cybersafetynet.biz/gmail.com. You clicked the link and wound up at http://cybersafetynet.biz/gmail.com while expecting http://gmail.com.
2. The email had an unnecessary sense of urgency. Why *exactly* do we have to reset a password within 24 hours? That unnecessary sense of urgency is a red flag.
3. The email had awkward grammar. "acquire your email within 24 hours or your account will be exterminated" is comical on two fronts. I do not ***acquire*** email. I read email. Perhaps you do too. My account will be ***exterminated***. Why didn't they say ***deleted***? Awkward grammar indicates that someone who does not speak North American English wrote the email.

You also need to be street smart. The link took you to http://cybersafetynet.biz/gmail.com. Why exactly did you click a link? Was it because you were late, frustrated or distracted?

Why email?

Brad Cracker

That is a valid question. I could have created fake (spoofed) pages at Amazon, eBay or *The New York Times*. Why an email service? Why Gmail?

I am making a few assumptions.

1. You use your Gmail address and password elsewhere. As soon as I learn them (I mean, as soon as you naively share them with me), I have a username and password I can try elsewhere.
2. I can initiate password reset requests elsewhere. Suppose I want to hack into your Amazon account. I would visit Amazon and try logging in as you. If I fail, I ask Amazon to send me a password reset link ***to your Gmail account***. Seeing that I have your Gmail address and password, I access your Gmail, read Amazon's password reset email and reset the password to one of my choosing. I win. You lose.
3. You won't suspect this happened. Remember, you were successful accessing your Gmail ***on your second attempt***. You were late, frustrated and distracted. You

clicked a link you should not have clicked. You also failed to access your Gmail on the first attempt. Successfully accessing Gmail on your second attempt may be the first successful thing you've done today.

Could have been avoided

I have your password. This could have been avoided if you kept security top-of-mind and vetted that link. That's why Mark feels security awareness training is your best line of defense. Mark will preach about security awareness training later. Just remember that good security awareness training for you and your staff — and keeping security top-of-mind — make my job harder.

Care for a USB memory stick?

Although I chose email as my attack vector, I could have dropped USB memory sticks in your parking lot. These can hold anything, including my malware. Perhaps you find one by your front door, feel good about getting a free USB memory stick, go into work and plug it into your computer.

"No way," you may say. "Nobody would be that naive." I beg to differ. A few years back, Mark attended a security conference at Microsoft's Redmond, Washington campus. The Sunday morning 8:30 AM speaker announced he "dropped" 40 USB memory sticks at random places throughout the convention hall. This was a conference of computer security people like Mark, who are supposed to be ultra conservative. They would never intentionally compromise their security.

Figure 8: Do not put random USB memory sticks in your computer. They may contain malware

The speaker also revealed attendees inserted 19 of those USB memory sticks into kiosk computers and started recording keystrokes. Of those 19 that made it into computers, 14 recorded website addresses, usernames and passwords. The malware he put on these USB memory sticks also sent a log back to the author, who used this as an example of how we all need to keep security top-of-mind.

I'm sure you've seen ransom USB memory sticks at random places. Next time you find one, let it sit. It may be a trap, like what the Microsoft conference speaker laid, for gullible users.

Mark Anthony

One of my clients receives USB memory sticks almost every day. I set up a computer that has three virus and malware protection apps. It connects to his internet router, outside of his firewall. Even though this computer is under his roof, the firewall protects his computers from any malware that may travel from a USB memory stick to the computer. He trained staff to take all inbound USB memory sticks, insert them into the testing workstation and scan them with all three virus protection and malware apps. After verifying the USB memory sticks are clean, employees can insert them into their own workstations and copy data from them.

Pwned

You are now pwned

Mark Anthony

Yes, I spelled that right. Someone who should not have your email and password does. Brad pwned you. Troy Hunt created the website https://haveibeenpwned.com/ to help you "check if you have an account that has been compromised in a data breach." I'd say Brad's fake Gmail login page ***helped*** facilitate a data breach. The actual data breach is Brad using your Gmail address and password at a website where you conduct business. Brad already mentioned Amazon. He may buy some TVs with your account.

That is one way a pwn happens. Another is your business partner getting hacked. A business partner is a company or website where you conduct business. I do business with Microsoft. Therefore, Microsoft is a business partner.

HaveIbeenpwned

Let's get back to Troy Hunt's website, https://haveibeenpwned.com/. You may be super careful with your passwords. You may vet links. You may use different passwords at different websites. You may employ multi factor authentication. You may follow all my advice on protecting your identity. Bravo to you. Your business partners probably don't.

"Your business partners probably don't." Did that scare you? It scared me when I first learned. Some data breaches make the national news. I am writing this section exactly one week after Honda of America disclosed that an unsecured database was available online.

https://www.bleepingcomputer.com/news/security/honda-exposes-26-000-records-of-north-american-customers/ reported "automotive giant Honda exposed roughly 26,000 vehicle owner records containing personally identifiable information (PII) of North American customers.

Honda's security team in Japan promptly secured the publicly accessible server within just a few hours after being contacted by Security Discovery researcher Bob Diachenko on December 12.

The researcher discovered the database on December 11 and was able to access the data without authentication after the BinaryEdge internet-connected device search engine indexed the database on December 4."

What exactly does "without authentication" mean? You guessed it. No password required.

I own a Honda.

If you want to discover your pwned status in general, take a deep breath and type your email address at https://haveibeenpwned.com/ then press (Enter).

These entries are not your fault. We can blame security staffers at these companies for their negligence. Here are my findings for my oldest email account, mark@cameronparkcomputer.com.

> ***What does "without authentication" mean?***
> *A) The computer scans your eyeball.*
> *B) Write your passwords on Post-It notes.*
> *C) No password required.*
>
> *Correct answer: C.*

1. Adobe. **Compromised data:** Email addresses, Password hints, Passwords, Usernames
2. Apollo. Who are they? I have not done business with Apollo. Perhaps a vendor of mine contracted out services to Apollo or rebranded Apollo. **Compromised data:** Email addresses, Employers, Geographic locations, Job titles, Names, Phone numbers, Salutations, Social media profiles.
3. Data & Leads. Once again, who are they? **Compromised data:** Email addresses, Employers, IP addresses, Job titles, Names, Phone numbers, Physical addresses.
4. Data Enrichment Exposure From PDL Customer. Once again, who are they? **Compromised data:** Email addresses, Employers, Geographic locations, Job titles, Names, Phone numbers, Social media profiles
5. Evite. Yes, I have used Evite. Most of my Evite activity happens under a Yahoo account. Only one or two invitations came through mark@cameronparkcomputer.com. **Compromised data:** Dates of birth, Email addresses, Genders, Names, Passwords, Phone numbers, Physical addresses
6. Exactis. Once again, who are they? **Compromised data:** Credit status information, Dates of birth, Education levels, Email addresses, Ethnicities, Family structure, Financial investments, Genders, Home ownership statuses, Income levels, IP addresses, Marital statuses, Names, Net worths, Occupations, Personal interests, Phone numbers, Physical addresses, Religions, Spoken languages.
7. Forbes. **Compromised data:** Email addresses, Passwords, User website URLs, Usernames
8. LinkedIn. **Compromised data:** Email addresses, Passwords.
9. Netprospex. Once again, who are they? **Compromised data:** Email addresses, Employers, Job titles, Names, Phone numbers, Physical addresses.

10. Online Spambot. Once again, who are they? **Compromised data:** Email addresses, Passwords.
11. River City Media Spam List. Once again, who are they? **Compromised data:** Email addresses, IP addresses, Names, Physical addresses.
12. ShareThis. **Compromised data:** Dates of birth, Email addresses, Names, Passwords.
13. Trik Spam Botnet. Once again, who are they? **Compromised data:** Email addresses.
14. Tumblr. **Compromised data:** Email addresses, Passwords.
15. Verifications.io. Once again, who are they? **Compromised data:** Dates of birth, Email addresses, Employers, Genders, Geographic locations, IP addresses, Job titles, Names, Phone numbers, Physical addresses.
16. Whitepages. I know who they are but have not done business with them. **Compromised data:** Email addresses, Names, Passwords.

This list comes from https://haveibeenpwned.com/. Several others either did not contain this email address or are too recent for inclusion. This would include big breaches at Adobe Systems, Canva, Capital One, Equifax, Facebook, first America Corporation, Friend Finder Networks, Heartland, Marriott International, Massive American Business Hack, Mobile TeleSystems, Quora, Target, Truecaller, Under Armour, Yahoo and Zynga. I am listing only data breaches with over 100 Million records, from https://en.wikipedia.org/wiki/List_of_data_breaches.

How many of those services look familiar? If you do business with any of them, you have some cleanup work to do.

Youhavebeenpwned and here's your homework

Have you been pawned? Yes, you probably have. Visit https://haveibeenpwned.com/ and https://en.wikipedia.org/wiki/List_of_data_breaches. Find business partners you recognize. List 10. Go to those sites. Login and change passwords or initiate password resets and then change passwords.

HaveIbeenpwned		
Website	Username and Password	Date Completed

You probably did not do the homework

Brad Cracker

Wasn't that cute? Mark thinks you have nothing else to do. Drop everything, look for websites that have been breached and reset your passwords. I bet you did not get through half of them. Too many websites. Too many passwords. Too little time. Why not just create a simple password and use it everywhere? That's what some people do. That makes my job easier.

Passwords

Simple and popular passwords

I read once that 40% of hacked company data is hacked from external sources. This 40% would be people on the internet and outside your company who have no business looking at your data. They browse your data. They use your data to their advantage. They sell your data. Guess how the remaining 60% of company data is hacked. Yes...from internal sources. This would include people in your company who get their hands-on information that they should not be able to see. The easiest path is to learn, guess or crack a password. I've seen some people set passwords that are extremely easy to remember. They are also easy to crack.

PCMagazine published a list of the top 10 most popular passwords at http://www.pcmag.com/article2/0,2817,2113976,00.asp, displayed in the following table so you can circle any that you use (and will change quickly). They say: *If you recognize yours, you may as well hand over your wallet or purse to the first person you see on the street.*

password	**123456**	**qwerty**	abc123	letmein
monkey	myspace1	password1	link182	(your first name)

That list was from 2007 and appeared in Mark's first book *How to Make Computer Systems Work for You* ©2010. "But Brad," you may say. "We're not in 2007 anymore." I agree we're not in 2007, but password creativity may still be there.

https://www.techspot.com/news/83279-worst-passwords-year-bad-youd-expect.html published a similar list for 2019.

123456	123456789	**qwerty**	**password**	1234567
12345678	12345	iloveyou	111111	123123

I bolded passwords that made the top 10 list both in 2007 and 2019.

Harvesting passwords

Mark Anthony

So far, we've been talking about single passwords. Let's go one step further. You volunteered your Gmail address and password at the spoofed Gmail login page. That generated an email with your Gmail address and password. Brad can harvest hundreds or even thousands of passwords.

"No way," you may say. "That would be too much work."

I do not think so. The folks at https://pastebin.com/gVs0cbXW published email credentials online.[i] I am pasting 19 entries here, along with the daphneprancer@gmail.com example from (above). These are following the convention of emailaddress: **password**.

emailaddress: password	emailaddress: password
dannygitar@gmail.com: **rockass**	herliviasandra@Yahoo.co.id: **herlyherly**
gatewayrealty1@Yahoo.com: **whiskers**	dannypiojoso@hotmail.com: **satan666**
h.julian1998@gmail.com: **haju1711**	gieddmfs@gmail.com: **tg021870**
hanson0219@gmail.com: **scman219**	herry.tanuwijaya@gmail.com: **tanu123wijaya**
imagbfan@live.com: **tuffcase**	jim.wanamakerii@gmail.com: **Landoman1**
daphneprancer@gmail.com: **2018Prius**	e.schoebi@bluewin.ch: **sabiner04**
javonquincygio@Yahoo.co.id: **antabaru**	gersonmoracid@gmail.com: **ger27021988**
irenaalivita@Yahoo.com: **123456**	intanjacob@gmail.com: **pawpawpanda7885**
hello@natashaestelle.com: **FN050763s**	kim.d.turnage@gmail.com: **scanner**
kballardsmith@gmail.com: **lorensmith**	kblock39@gmail.com: **kb9298kb**

With her 123456 password, I feel irenaalivita@Yahoo.com should not be allowed internet access until she creates more complex passwords and finds a way to manage them. She's almost begging to become a victim.

A password solution

We have too many passwords. Keeping track of them mentally or on Post-It notes does not work. Keeping them in a Microsoft Word document is also troublesome. If you change a password and fail to update the document, then the record becomes wrong. Next time you go to that website and use the password in your Microsoft Word document, it won't work. You did not update the document.

> ***How are you managing passwords?***
> *A) An online password manager, such as LastPass.*
> *B) Post-It notes and random papers.*
> *C) Ha Ha Mark. You must be kidding.*
>
> *Correct answer (what you should be doing): A*

Several companies have solutions. I use LastPass, which lets you create a vault that holds all your passwords. You don't have to remember what LastPass stores in the vault. You only have to remember the master password to access the vault. LastPass therefore promotes itself as the **LastPass**word you have to remember. Cute name? Yes. Yes. Yes.

Download and install the LastPass toolbar from http://lastpass.com and create your account. The password you set becomes your master password. When you visit a website and login, LastPass asks if you want to save a record for that website. I usually say yes. You can go back and edit that record.

You can get a free account and access your vault through http://lastpass.com and a toolbar. I upgraded my account to Premium status. $3/month helps me **not** have to think about passwords. My Twitter record looks like this.

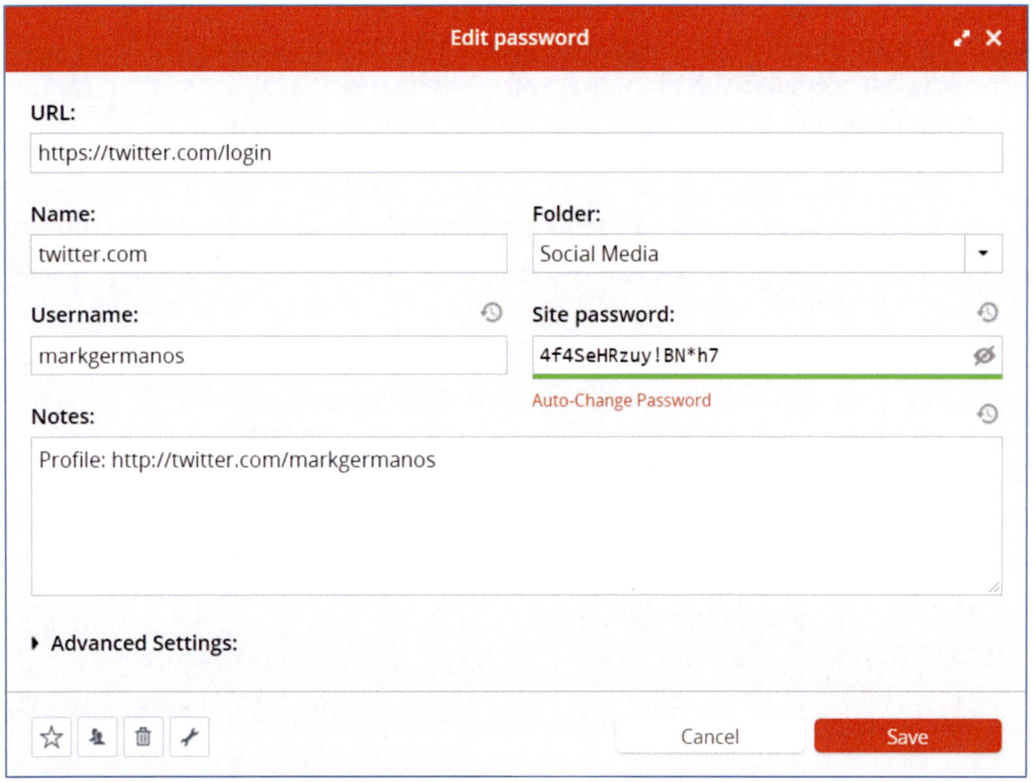

Figure 9: A standard LastPass record

After creating a few records, I started creating folders to help organize them. The Social Media folder has a name of my choosing. I also did not set the **4f4SeHRzuy!BN*h7** password. Only a computer could set one that cryptic. I was at Twitter one day and I manually reset my password. I let LastPass propose alternate passwords. I chose **4f4SeHRzuy!BN*h7**, updated my Twitter password and saved the new password in LastPass.

Don't bother trying to login to my Twitter account with that password. I changed it after proofreading the previous paragraph. Changing the password within LastPass took less than 30 seconds.

LastPass lets you create a hierarchy. In the same manner your organization has a CEO who delegates to various department managers, LastPass lets you build teams and add or remove users. https://www.lastpass.com/team-password-manager lists these benefits:

1. Instantly add and remove team members.
2. Safely share passwords with others.
3. Give each employee their own vault for safeguarding passwords.
4. Store digital records: Wi-Fi logins, software licenses, employee IDs, and more.
5. Set security controls and restrictions based on your team's needs.

The biggest challenge is compiling all your current passwords. What you remember, what you save on Post-It notes, what you save in a web browser when it asks if you want to save the password after successfully logging in... These all go into LastPass.

I have an obvious preference for LastPass. Anything is better than nothing. Choose one online password manager and go to work adding your passwords.

Anything is better than nothing

"Anything is better than nothing?" you may ask. Yes. You read that right. Here's why I say that.

A man walks into a hardware store and says to an employee, "I need to pound a nail into the wall. What do I do?" The employee walks the man to the hammer display and says, "Here. Buy this red hammer. Use the red hammer to pound the nail into the wall." He turns around and walks away.

Five minutes later, another employee walks up and asks the man if he needs any help. The man says, "I need to pound a nail into the wall. What do I do?" The employee says, "Here. Buy this blue hammer. Use the blue hammer to pound the nail into the wall." He turns around and walks away.

Five minutes later, the man is looking at green hammers. He then looks at the blue hammers and the red hammers. He throws up his arms in disgust, cusses and walks out of the store.

It doesn't matter what color the hammer is. He just wants to pound a nail into the wall.

Password homework

Remember when I wrote "The biggest challenge is..." slightly before the hammer story? That is your homework. I am presenting the same table I presented in the Haveibeenpwnd section. This time, you log the website, your username and your password. Look for Post-It notes, check your email, log into websites and see if you remember the passwords. Document them here when you do.

Password Manager		
Website	Username and Password	Date Completed

But wait there's more! Visit https://lastpass.com and create a personal (free account). Follow the prompts to create the account and start entering records.

When I embraced LastPass as my exclusive password management tool and entered all my passwords into it, I had 218 records. You will probably need a second page. Here you go.

Password Manager		
Website	Username and Password	Date Completed

Multi Factor Authentication

Say hello to Multi Factor Authentication

Let's present another LastPass record. This one is for Sophos, a security company. I use their mobile product to centrally manage smart phones and tablets.

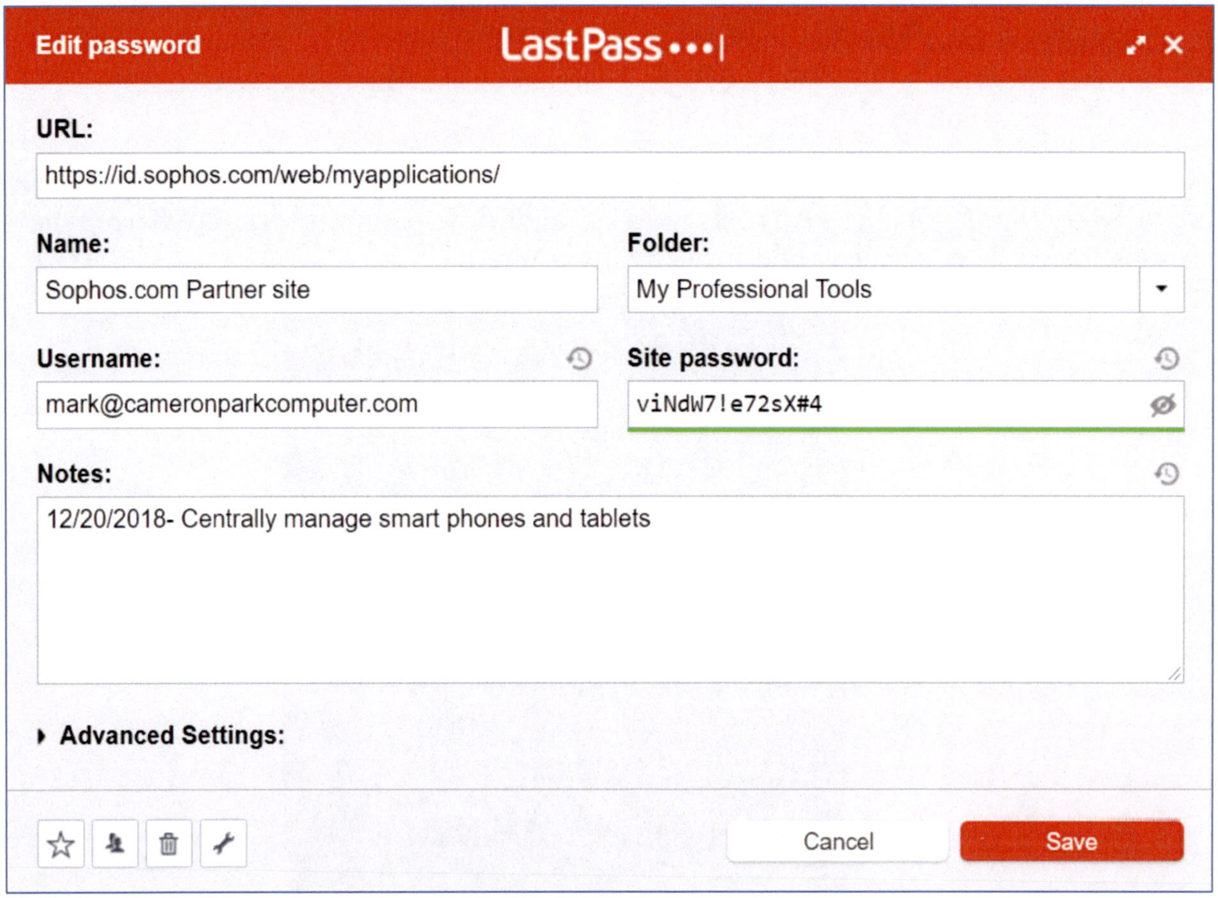

Figure 10: I need more than a password to get into this site

I am sharing this record because I have enabled MFA (Multi Factor Authentication) at Sophos. Multi Factor Authentication is an added security measure guarding your access to personal information.

Here's some background to authentication. When you try connecting to a website, the website challenges you to prove who you are. I visit Twitter and say I am markgermanos. Twitter responds, "Uh huh, prove it." I provide my password and gain access into Twitter. I used one factor, my password, to access Twitter.

One factor is not enough, especially when people reuse passwords or choose simple passwords. Webmasters encourage and sometimes enforce multi factor authentication. Multi Factor Authentication works on the premise of:

1. **What you know**. For example, I know a website password.
2. **Who you are**. For example, my fingerprints, facial scans and retinal scans are unique.
3. **What you have**. For example, I have an iPhone that receives texts on a mobile number I provide to my vendors.

Twitter authenticates me on one factor, my password. Sophos authenticates me on two factors, my password and a six-digit PIN Sophos sends me every time I try logging into Sophos. My most recent PIN was ***297734***. I am happy sharing that here because PINs expire after 30 seconds.

Microsoft authenticates me on two factors. I log into https://portal.office.com quite often. Every time I do, Microsoft texts me a six-digit PIN. I am comfortable sharing the six most recent here because they have already expired.

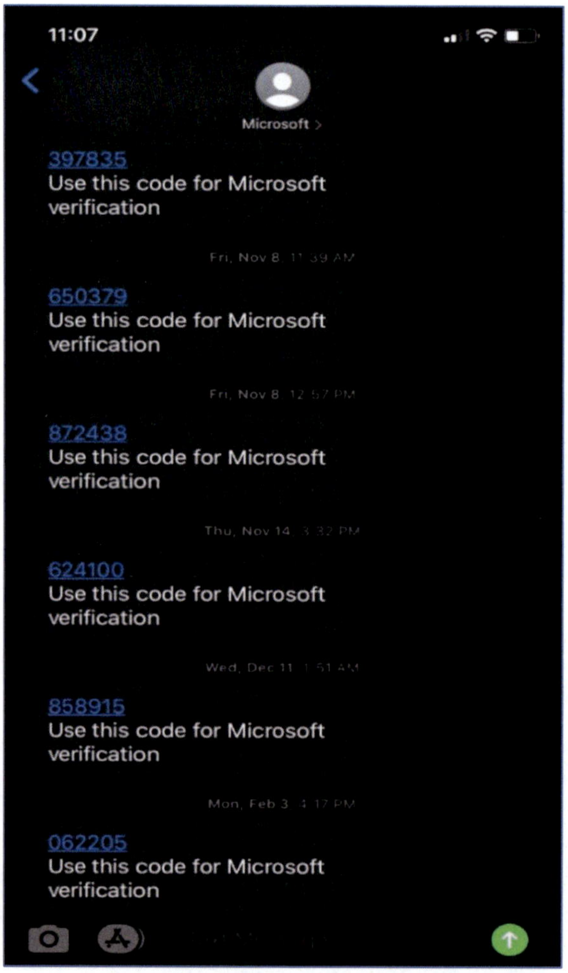

Figure 11: Microsoft requires a password and a PIN

Multi Factor Authentication is not universal. Several websites simply do not mandate Multi Factor Authentication. My theory is...too much user resistance. I have some experience with user resistance.

Last year, a client tasked me with deploying Multi Factor Authentication on 103 mailboxes at Microsoft Office 365. This was part of a project the client informed me was my top priority. I went to work scheduling sessions with users, some local and some remote, to enforce Multi Factor Authentication. Most users eagerly cooperated and appreciated the extra security measure. Others resisted. They questioned why this was necessary. They scheduled appointments and then stood me up. They did not respond to email.

One user ignored my calls and stood me up one time too many. I sensed she was not using her corporate email. I changed her email password, turned on Multi Factor Authentication and set my cell number as her mobile number. She did not notice any change for 65 days.

When attempting to access a website, the website can challenge you based on:

A) What you know (e.g. password).

B) Who you are (e.g. fingerprints).

C) What you have (e.g. phone).

D) All of the above.

Correct answer: D.

I blogged about Multi Factor Authentication. My blog entries first appeared at https://cameronparkcomputer.com. One argues in favor of Multi Factor Authentication and the other argues against. I blogged about 2 Factor Authentication, which involves two factors. Multi Factor Authentication involves ***at least*** two factors.[ii]

Say YES to 2-Factor Authentication

2-factor Authentication helps protect your identity.

You should deploy 2-factor Authentication. This increases your security and reduces your chances of becoming an identity theft victim. Most services encourage 2-factor Authentication and let you deploy it at no additional cost.

How it looks in real life.

Figure 12: 2-factor Authentication increases your security at no additional cost

Daisy runs a dental office in Folsom, CA. Keeping the practice up and running is her top priority. She runs most of her patient, insurance and vendor communications through her Gmail account. She deploys 2-factor Authentication with the steps at https://myaccount.google.com/signinoptions/two-step-verification/enroll-welcome. She keeps her smartphone nearby. She knows that when she logs into her Gmail account, or any Google service for that matter, Google will send her a six-digit code.

She goes to work one Monday morning. She logs into her Gmail account then receives a text message. It reveals the current six-digit code. She enters that into the Google PIN prompt and reads her email. Pretty simple, after the initial setup and overcoming the "am I doing this right?" doubts.

Daisy realizes that 2-factor Authentication resides on a) what you know and b) what you have. Daisy knows her Gmail password. Daisy has a PIN that Google sends to her smartphone.

Daisy has 2-factor Authentication. She knows that even if someone guesses or steals her Gmail password, they do not have the PIN and they do not have her smart phone. It works for Daisy.

The benefit.

Daisy works hard. She makes sure the practice's security meets modern standards. She maintains strong passwords and protects client data. She also knows if something is complex, she might as well contract out the work to someone who does security work and can get it working right, the first time. Setting up 2-factor Authentication is not something to take lightly.

Say NO to 2-Factor Authentication

You do not need 2-factor Authentication.

2-factor Authentication helps improve your security and reduces your chance of becoming an identity theft victim. I have already written why you should deploy 2-factor Authentication. In this post, I shall play the Devil's Advocate. ***Don't*** do it.

What happens if you don't do it?

Figure 13: 2-factor Authentication increases your security at no additional cost

Allen does not see things the same way network consultants do. He decides that since he has been running his business without 2-factor Authentication for 20 years, he does not need it now. He thinks it is a scheme for computer guys to make life more complex and generate more billable work. Sad but true, that is what Allen thinks.

One day, Allen opens his Gmail and sees order confirmations for TVs, DVRs and other consumer items. They were all shipped to an address in Moscow. Most came from Amazon. He stands up and yells, "Hey, somebody hacked my accounts. Not only did they get my email, but they also got into my Amazon.com and Buy.com. I had a good password of ***abcdeABCDE***. How did this happen?"

It happened because Allen used one password at several sites. He now has the inconvenient task of notifying his vendors to cancel the orders. He also has to set new passwords at every site where he was using ***abcdeABCDE*** as the password. He rethinks the 2-factor Authentication idea his friend recommended last week. Maybe network consultants ***do*** have good ideas. Hmmmmm.

Why bother?

2-factor Authentication increases your security and protects you from a password thief. Someone can steal or guess your password but still be unable to login to your Gmail. I use Gmail as an example here, but I've seen several services deploy this. Learn how to use 2-factor Authentication. It increases your security at no additional cost.

The Wikipedia administrators learned this the hard way. They report, "It is **really important** for users with advanced rights to keep their account secure. In November 2016, a number of Wikipedia administrators (including the founder, Jimbo Wales) had their accounts compromised, which were then used to vandalise (sic) the encyclopedia. As well as causing widespread disruption, the affected administrators' accounts were locked so they couldn't do anything until it was beyond doubt, they had regained control."

Authentication Apps

So far, I've been talking about websites sending you text messages. That is one way to enable Multi Factor Authentication. Another is to use an authentication application. I've seen several. Google Authenticator and Microsoft Authenticator are the big names. Both have no cost.

When you sign into a website where you have enabled Multi Factor Authentication and enrolled a device, you check the app and enter the current code. Make it quick. Codes refresh every 30 seconds.

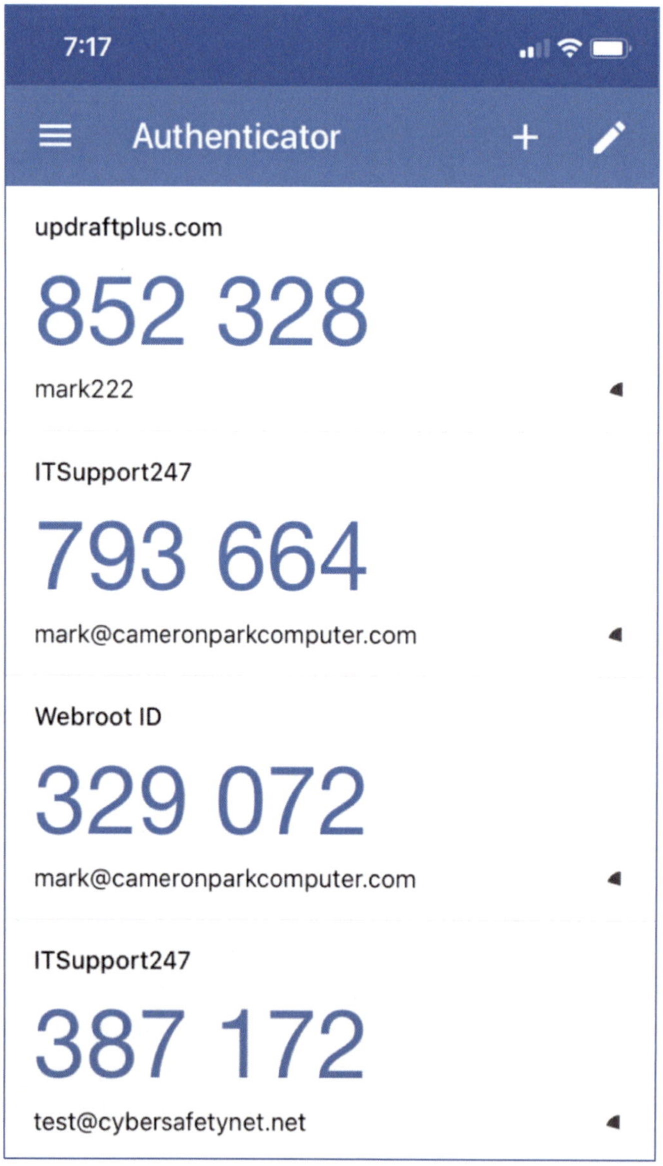

Figure 14: Multi Factor Authentication codes refresh every 30 seconds

Here are the websites where I a) have enabled Multi Factor Authentication and b) chose Google Authenticator, as opposed to text messaging, as the conduit.

1. Updraftplus. This service backs up websites I host.
2. ITSupport247. This service lets me remotely manage computers.
3. Webroot. This is the virus protection I support.

Text messages or an Authentication app?

Which is better? Having a website send you text messages or update an authentication app, like Google Authenticator? I've heard loyalists promote one at the expense of the other. I hereby refer you to my "Anything is better than nothing" story on page 20 again.

Multi Factor Authentication homework

I am sure you noticed "homework" is two four-letter words put together. Here is your new homework assignment. Document 10 websites and establish Multi Factor Authentication at all of them. Some call it 2-Factor Authentication.

Establish Multi Factor Authentication		
Website	Username and Password	Date Completed

Establish Multi Factor Authentication		
Website	Username and Password	Date Completed

Convenience vs. Security

40,000-foot view

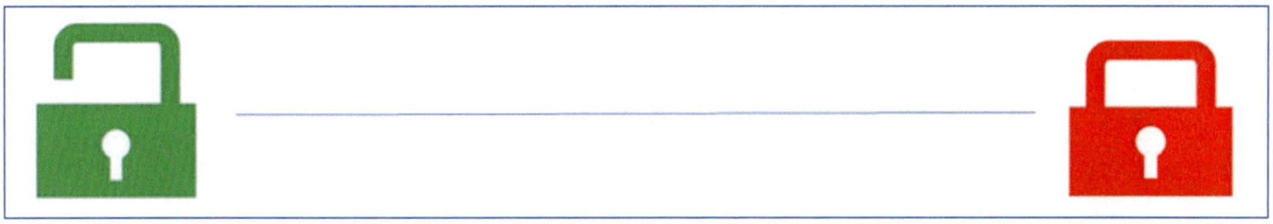

Figure 15: We all live on a spectrum, with 100% convenience on one end and 100% security on the other

You will get hacked. It's a matter of time. Internet thieves will find you. They will harvest your credit card numbers, social security numbers and passwords. The compile this information into Microsoft Excel workbooks and sell it on the dark web. What you do is not important. What you have, and what they can sell, is. We all live on a spectrum. On one end we find convenience and on the other end we find security.

100% convenience

If you choose 100% convenience, you keep computers on and logged in all the time. You have a near-field connection that lets you pay for gasoline and other retail purchases without removing anything from your wallet and you have one password you use everywhere. This may even be *p@ssword*.

100% security

If you choose 100% security, you pay cash for everything and have a computer that does not talk to others. 100% security disqualifies using a computer in the first place. Why have a computer if it does not talk to any others?

100% security is not attainable

I am arguing 100% security is not attainable. We all live on a spectrum. What is the world's most closely guarded secret? I propose.... the secret formula of Coca Cola.

The Coca Cola corporation would agree. They keep the secret formula in a vault in downtown Atlanta. I visited Atlanta's World of Coca-Cola museum last year and approached the vault that holds the secret recipe. Coca Cola stores the recipe there, in a vault and assigns a security guard to the vault entrance.

What we don't know is:

1. Is the formula in an electronic format or is it still on paper and sealed in an airtight box, like our nation's *Declaration of Independence*?
2. Is this the only copy? Do they have a redundant copy somewhere else?
3. How is Coca Cola protecting this from fire, flood or theft?
4. Who checks the vault to make sure the formula is still there?
5. Why did the beautiful security guard leave her post and take my picture?

Figure 16: Who guards the vault containing the secret formula of Coca Cola while the beautiful security guard takes my picture?

We live somewhere in the middle

We are ***not*** using p@ssword as a password at every website and we are ***not*** storing our secrets in a vault, like Coca Cola does. We grant ourselves convenience and with that convenience, we assume risk.

Attractive targets

We are rich Americans

When I say that on stage, people roll their eyes and mumble “Ahhhh, he has not seen my mortgage payment, does not pay my bills or have kids to feed. He is not talking about me.” Yes, I am talking about you.

A rich American” is an American who:

1. Carries a credit card.
2. Lives in a home larger than 800 square feet.
3. Drives a car that starts on the first try.

Figure 17: To qualify as a rich American, you need a credit card, a house larger than 800 square feet and a car that starts on the first try

I’m not setting the bar too high, now am I? What you are is not important. What you have is. You have a home. I have heard of house theft, where thieves redirect mortgage statements, the owner stops paying, the home falls into foreclosure and the thief buys it from the bank. Scary? Yes. It happens.

You have a credit card. I’ve seen people buy credit card numbers and purchase items for their benefit. If you ever had an unknown charge on a credit card statement and learned the transaction is for something you did not buy or something was shipped to somewhere you have never visited, you know what this is.

You have a car. Thieves in the San Francisco Bay Area steal cars and drive them directly to the port and onto a ship. Sometimes they want cars intact. Sometimes they want to scrap cars and sell them for parts. Regardless, a car that starts on the first try is something you have, and a thief wants.

Hover technique

Think back to the opening series. Brad presented a fake Gmail login page. You got there by inattentively clicking a link. You assumed the link was taking you to Gmail but in reality, the link took you elsewhere. You could have prevented this by doing my hover trick.

Move your mouse pointer over a link but ***don't*** click it. Your computer presents a balloon box telling you where you will end up ***if*** you click the link. My earlier example of http://gmail.com actually takes you to http://cybersafetynet.biz/gmail.com. Hovering over the link reveals where the link will take you.

Figure 18: Hover before clicking

What a phishing attack looks like

https://en.wikipedia.org/wiki/Phishing defines phishing as "the fraudulent attempt to obtain sensitive information such as usernames, passwords and credit card details by disguising oneself as a trustworthy entity in an electronic communication. Typically carried out by email spoofing or instant messaging, it often directs users to enter personal information at a fake website which matches the look and feel of the legitimate site." The email I just described qualifies as a phishing attack.

Phishing emails are SPAM with a sinister intention. Look for three traits when determining if an email is a phish attempt. Only one of three is necessary.

1. Awkward grammar.
2. Unnecessary sense of urgency.
3. Links that do not make sense.

Let's review one that appeared in my inbox one day. You've probably received some with similar traits.

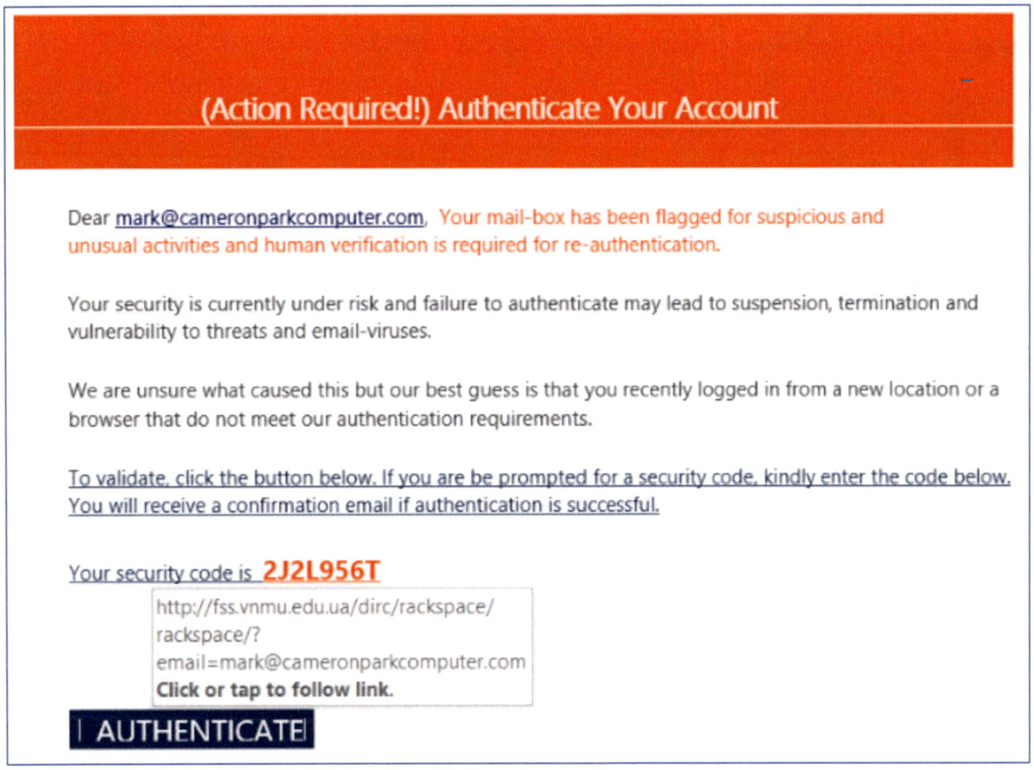

Figure 19: Our best guess...

1. Awkward grammar. The "We are unsure what caused this but our best guess is..." is awkward and humorous. Did they run out of ideas because someone's caffeine buzz faded?
2. Unnecessary sense of urgency? I did not find one here.
3. Link that does not make sense. I hovered over the AUTHENTICATE link to reveal where I will end up if I click the link. The address **fss.vnmu.edu.ua** tells us the server is in .ua. Ukraine.

Sometimes the scammers leverage current issues and fears. I am proofreading this section three days after California Governor Gavin Newsom placed California on lockdown. People are nervous. People are afraid. People are looking for information.

Scammers are leveraging Coronavirus. My business partner, Sophos, published a Coronavirus phishing attack sample at https://nakedsecurity.sophos.com/2020/02/05/coronavirus-safety-measures-email-is-a-phishing-scam/. Those who leverage a disaster like the Coronavirus outbreak as an attack vector are truly the scum of the world. Here is a specimen of their tactics.

Figure 20: The scammer didn't bother to proofread their work

Remember when I wrote "awkward grammar" on the previous page? This phishing email has both awkward grammar and an obvious spelling mistake. What exactly is "fever,coughcshortness"?

> ***Traits of phishing emails:***
> *A) Awkward grammar.*
> *B) Unnecessary sense of urgency.*
> *C) Links that do not make sense.*
> *D) At least one of the above.*
>
> *Correct answer: D.*

Vet the short links

I'm sure you agree that website addresses are not always honest. My earlier example of http://gmail.com actually takes you to http://cybersafetynet.biz/gmail.com. Hovering over the link reveals where the link will take you.

Figure 21: Hover before clicking

Sometimes we see short links that someone created after realizing a long link would be nearly impossible for someone to remember and would wrap across multiple lines. The link https://cybersafetynet.net/office-depot-fake-malware-scans-unneeded-300-services-2/ takes up too much space. It sure would be convenient if I could present a shortened link http://alturl.com/zk94i. I can save space. I can also conceal the destination.

There are multiple services that create short links. The big names are Bit.ly, Google, TinyURL, Twitter, WordPress and the service I used for this example, ShortURL. Generating short URLs, or web page addresses, is big business. I Googled "short URL" and Google presented more than 2.4 billion results.

What do you do when you see a short URL link? They are even more concealing than the gmail.com example. I have some good news. You can expand a short URL to see where you will go if you click the link.

Take my shortened URL http://alturl.com/zk94i and enter (or copy and paste it) at http://expandurl.com/. Expand URL reveals the true destination.

Figure 22: Short URLs save space. They can also hide your true destination. Vet short URLs before clicking them

This helps you determine where you will end up if you click a link. Do not let short URLs earn more trust than others. The link http://alturl.com/zk94i could have redirected you to...any sinister site. Some hackers use short URLs because they save space and conceal their true destinations.

The true objective of phishing attacks is to entice you to click links you should not click. Just remember that good security awareness training for you and your staff, and keeping security top-of-mind, make the hackers' jobs harder.

Phishing traits homework

When was the last time you saw a suspicious email? Maybe you have an excellent SPAM filter. Outlook, as a client to my mark@cybersafetynet.net Office 365 account, has intercepted 351 messages during the past 29 days. Check your email. Look at some sample emails and document the sender, the subject line and the suspicious factors (awkward grammar, unnecessary sense of urgency and/or links that do not make sense). Look in your SPAM or Junk Email folder if you don't have enough in your Inbox.

Identifying phishing emails		
Sender	Subject line	Triggering factor

Hacking

How I hack

Brad Cracker

Mark keeps assigning you homework. He thinks you have nothing else to do. I know you're not doing it. I am counting on you to ***not*** do the homework and instead lazily click links that I send you. Mark's "keeping security top-of-mind and getting security awareness training" strategy is your best line of defense. If you're not doing the homework, you're probably not keeping security top-of-mind. I will find you.

Wikipedia.com at https://en.wikipedia.org/wiki/Security_hacker says "A security hacker is someone who explores methods for breaching defenses and exploiting weaknesses in a computer system or network…" A primary part of hacking is hiding your tracks. Make sure forensic investigators cannot find you. This is a game of cat and mouse.

Let's start simple and walk before we run.

Private browsing (incognito mode)

You can browse privately. Google describes private browsing at https://support.google.com/chrome/answer/7440301. It states: "Some information will not be seen or saved. Once you exit all your Incognito browsing windows, Chrome won't save:

1. Your browsing history.
2. Your cookies and site data.
3. Information you entered in forms.
4. Permissions you give websites.
5. To exit Incognito mode, close all Incognito windows."

"Great!" You may say. "Google Chrome is not saving my browsing history! My spouse cannot see where I've been online." You spouse and coworkers cannot see your history, but Google's search engine remembers. If someone seriously wanted to find out which websites you have visited, they could subpoena Google.

Google reports at https://transparencyreport.google.com/user-data/overview?user_requests_report_period=authority:US they received 12,902 subpoenas in January – June, 2019 for just the United States. This page continues: "Government agencies, courts, and parties in civil litigation regularly ask technology and communications companies to turn over user data. In this report, we disclose information about the number and type of requests we receive from governments."

Private browsing isn't as private as you thought, now is it?

VPN to...anywhere

We've learned private browsing is not private at all. If you try connecting to someone's server, the server and firewall logs record your IP address. You can redirect all your traffic through another location. You do that with a VPN application.

I use a VPN application called IPVanish. This lets me connect to various servers throughout the world. I briefly referred to this when I wrote "If your computer logs document my intrusion, they may report I was in Dubai, London or Reykjavik. Good luck finding me. I am in Sacramento" way back near the start. The list is much longer. With IPVanish, I can connect to 55 countries and choose multiple cities in most. The United States offerings include Ashburn, Atlanta, Boston, Charlotte, Chicago, Dallas, Denver, Houston, Las Vegas, Los Angeles, Miami, New Orleans, New York, Phoenix, San Jose and Seattle. Not sure, choose the default "Best Available City."

Figure 23: I am in London, according to anybody who reviews server or firewall logs

IPVanish is not the only VPN software out there. It is, however, the one I use. It's only $4/month at https://www.ipvanish.com/.

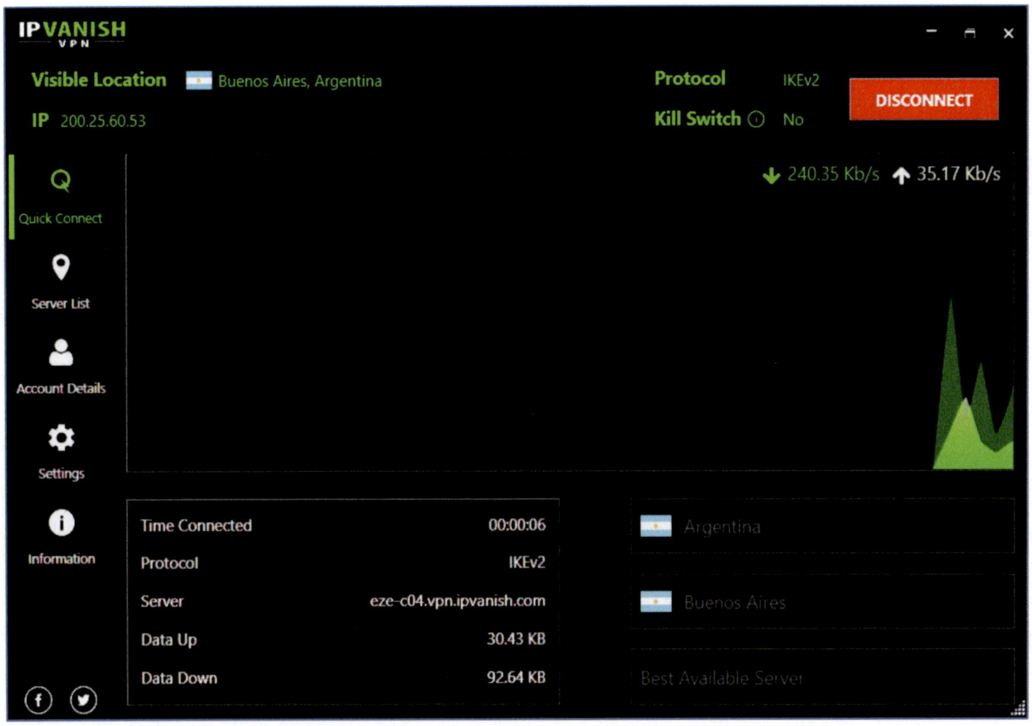

Figure 24: I am in Buenos Aires, according to anybody who reviews server or firewall logs

I can choose among 16 cities here in the US. How about Miami?

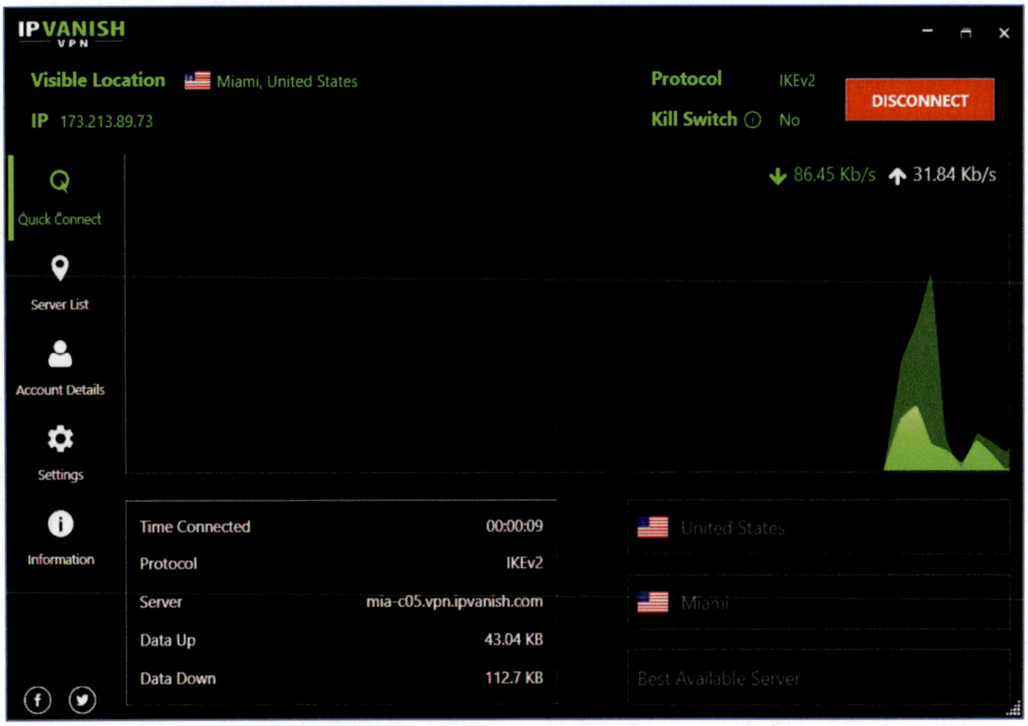

Figure 25: I am in Miami, according to anybody who reviews server or firewall logs

Let's see how this works. Suppose I want to connect to a firewall at 173.14.110.5[iii] from my current location and IP address of 73.192.190.118. The webmaster at 173.14.110.5 would geolocate my traffic from El Dorado Hills, California. Bravo to the folks at https://tools.keycdn.com/geo for reporting my location accurately.

We're trying to hide, remember? How about I launch IPVanish and connect to "Best Available City" and see what random city piggybacks my traffic. The winner is San Jose. The IPVanish server there allocates me 216.151.183.142

Let's go overseas. We're still trying to hide, remember? How about I launch IPVanish and connect to a city in Switzerland. The only option there is Zurich. The IPVanish server there allocates me 45.82.223.102.

What the target's firewall logs report

The network administrator at my target reviews firewall logs and sees failed logins from three different IPs. One is in El Dorado Hills; one is in San Jose and one is in Zurich.

I am in El Dorado Hills, California, slightly east of Sacramento.

He visits https://tools.keycdn.com/geo and searches for 73.192.190.118. He thinks the attacker is in El Dorado Hills.

Local Time	ID	Category	Priority	Message	Source	Destination	IP Protocol
20:38:25 Feb 10	30	Users	Alert	Administrator login denied due to bad credentials	73.192.190.118, 3516, X1	[redacted]	tcp
20:38:16 Feb 10	30	Users	Alert	Administrator login denied due to bad credentials	73.192.190.118, 3509, X1	[redacted]	tcp
20:37:45 Feb 10	30	Users	Alert	Administrator login denied due to bad credentials	73.192.190.118, 3500, X1	[redacted]	tcp
20:37:38 Feb 10	30	Users	Alert	Administrator login denied due to bad credentials	73.192.190.118, 3489, X1	[redacted]	tcp
20:37:29 Feb 10	30	Users	Alert	Administrator login denied due to bad credentials	73.192.190.118, 3469, X1	[redacted]	tcp

He visits https://tools.keycdn.com/geo and searches for 216.151.183.142. He thinks the attacker is in San Jose.

Local Time	ID	Category	Priority	Message	Source	Destination	IP Protocol
21:34:08 Feb 10	30	Users	Alert	Administrator login denied due to bad credentials	216.151.183.142, 7965, X1	[redacted]	tcp
21:34:00 Feb 10	30	Users	Alert	Administrator login denied due to bad credentials	216.151.183.142, 7941, X1	[redacted]	tcp

He visits https://tools.keycdn.com/geo and searches for 45.82.223.102. He thinks the attacker is in Zurich.

Local Time	ID	Category	Priority	Message	Source	Destination	IP Protocol
21:36:53 Feb 10	30	Users	Alert	Administrator login denied due to bad credentials	45.82.223.102, 8198, X1	[redacted]	tcp
21:36:37 Feb 10	30	Users	Alert	Administrator login denied due to bad credentials	45.82.223.102, 8166, X1	[redacted]	tcp
21:35:43 Feb 10	30	Users	Alert	Administrator login denied due to bad credentials	45.82.223.102, 8129, X1	[redacted]	tcp
21:35:29 Feb 10	30	Users	Alert	Administrator login denied due to bad credentials	45.82.223.102, 8096, X1	[redacted]	tcp

What the target's Windows logs report

Maybe you use Microsoft's Remote Desktop feature to connect to your workstation at work from...anywhere. Remote Desktop has been in Windows for 20 years at no extra cost. The network administrator at my target reviews the workstation's logs through Windows' Event Viewer. This screenshot is from my research honeypot.[iv]

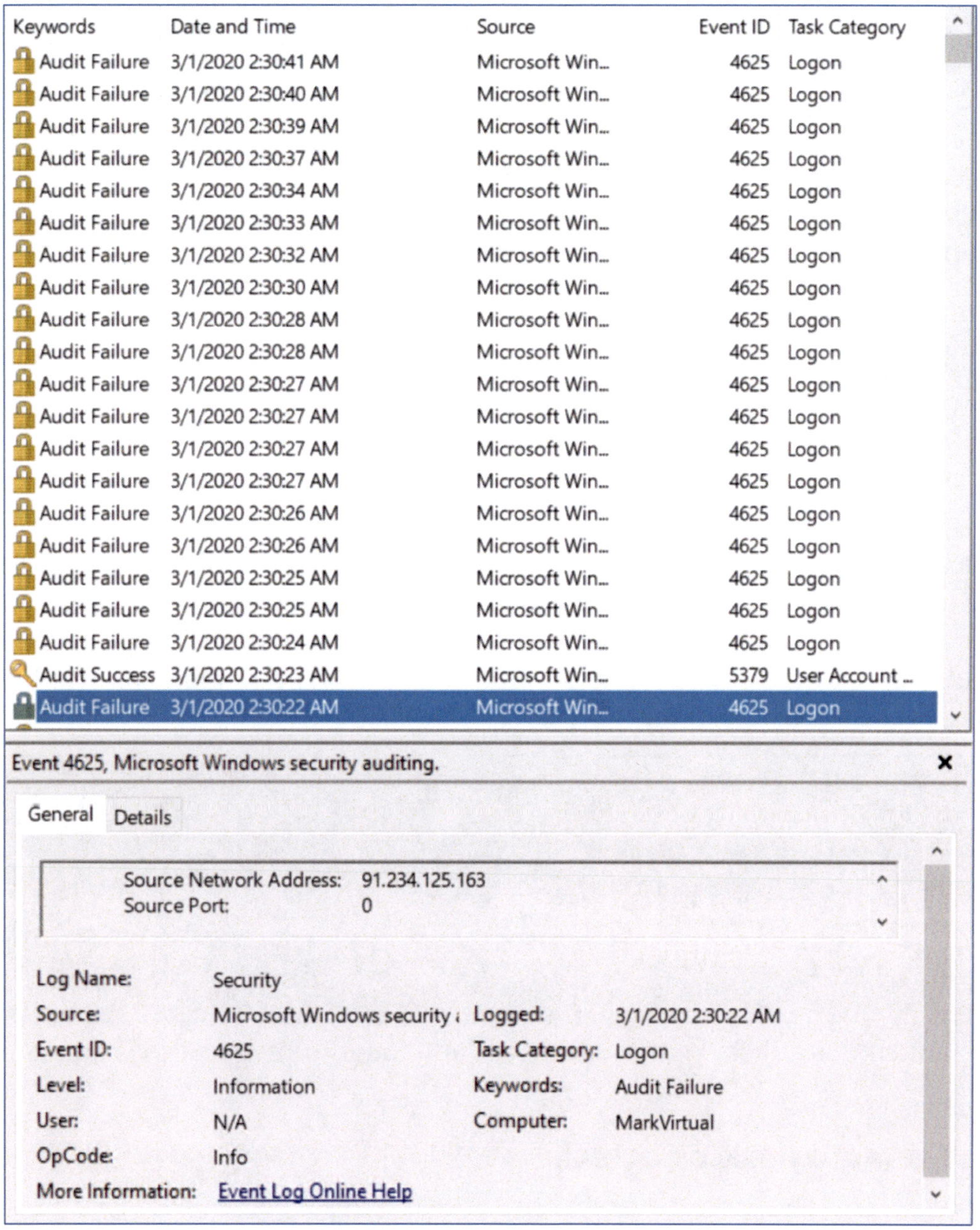

Figure 26: Someone is trying to login to this virtual machine at a ferocious pace

The unlucky soul who has to read these logs finds login attempts are international. My perusal shows login attempts from five IP addresses:

Attacks are international
211.72.1.31 in Taipei, Taiwan
24.142.48.215 in Dartmouth, Canada
87.147.195.55 in Olching, Germany
47.185.77.29 in Keller, Texas
91.234.125.163 is in Sosnicowice. Poland

Assuming it is one hacker who either employed a botnet (a series of computers simultaneously tasked with a large task) or is running multiple VPN connections; he will eventually succeed. He is trying to login with user accounts ***Administrator***, ***win*** and ***userid60307***. He will eventually succeed when:

1. ***Administrator***, ***win*** or ***userid60307*** use one of the simple passwords from page 17.
2. The hacker stumbles across the correct password in his wordlist.
3. Assuming Daphne Prancer uses this workstation, the hacker tries logging in as Daphne with the password ***2018Prius***.

This attack may go indefinitely. "How ferocious is this attack?" you may ask. Get ready for some math. I counted how many times Event ID 4625 occurred in one minute. The answer is...105. Yes, I counted 105 failed logins within 60 seconds. Do the math and you'll find a rate of 151,200 failed login attempts a day. Do more math and you'll find a rate of 55,188,000 attempts a year.

The hacker will eventually succeed
*105 * 60 = 6,300 attempts per hour*
*6300 * 24 = 151,200 attempts per day*
*151,200 * 365 = 55,188,000 attempts per year*

I did not launch this attack. I checked the logs and found someone else is doing my work for me.

Stop the remote desktop attack

Mark Anthony

Despite Brad's sinister intentions, he ***is*** good at math. Brad is right when he says the hacker will eventually succeed. When was the last time you checked the Security log on your computer? This computer is not behind a firewall that offers Intrusion Prevention features. If it were, the firewall would have identified and blocked this attack.

You stop this attack by blocking inbound traffic on port 3389 or turning off Remote Desktop in general. The computer will not respond to traffic on port 3389. The hacker will give up and take you off his list.

"But Mark, I need remote access to my work computer. You want to kill that?" No. I want you to get a decent business-class firewall, put your computer(s) behind it and find a more secure remote access solution. Tell your network manager you need a firewall that lets you filter inbound traffic and establish VPN connections with the firewall as an endpoint. If you're near Sacramento, call me. (530) 677-8864.

If you have a business-class firewall, you can block and log intrusion attempts. A Sacramento-area client has a SonicWall firewall and I have turned on the Intrusion Prevention service. This device has blocked 105,485 intrusion attempts in 18 days.

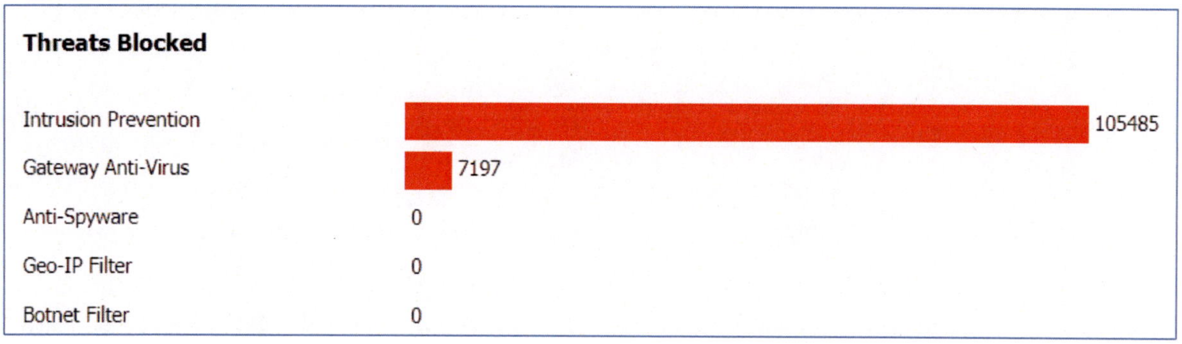

Figure 27: A business class firewall blocks intrusion attempts (this chart shows 18 days' activity)

VPN software is bad and VPN software is good

Brad Cracker

Mark just posted his phone number. Cute. I showed how I and other black hat hackers conceal our true location with VPN software. "It's bad, Brad. Bad. Bad. Bad," you may say. With my worldview and agenda, you can argue it is bad. I argue it is a tool and you use it for good or for bad. Your decision.

Mark Anthony

Despite Brad's agenda, VPN software can be used for good. You can go to a coffee shop and hop on the free WIFI. Before you launch any apps or visit any websites, launch the VPN software and initiate a connection. IPVanish lets you choose a target server but also lets you encrypt traffic. Anyone sniffing wireless traffic at the local coffee shop cannot make heads or tails from your traffic, because it is encrypted. Maybe that's why IPVanish is recommended by CNN, Mashable and PCMag.

You can also learn if your firewall or router allows inbound traffic. Visit https://canyouseeme.org/ and click the Check Port button. Leave the Port to Check field at ***80***, for now.

Figure 28: Are you allowing inbound (hackers') traffic?

Port ***80*** is for World Wide Web traffic. Port ***443*** is for *Secure* World Wide Web traffic. Port ***3389*** is for Remote Desktop traffic. Each internet-connected computer has 65,535 ports for inbound traffic.

Here's how I learned about ports. Suppose you are in a boat off the California coast. You have a full tank of gas. You can choose from 11 major California ports, spanning from San Diego to the North Coast. You can disembark at any port and still end up in California.

Getting back to your computer, you have 65,535 ports. Most are closed. If you enable Microsoft's Remote Desktop, you open port 3389. Hackers then see you have port 3389 open and can hammer away until they stumble across a valid username and password combination.

Open ports homework

1. Visit https://canyouseeme.org/.
2. Check ports 80 and 443. If they are open, call your network manager and ask why your computer is running a website.
3. Check port 3389. If this is open, tell your network manager you need a more secure tool that grants you remote access into this computer. Turn off Remote Desktop.

Hacking WordPress

Hacking into a WordPress website

Mark Anthony

I am choosing the WordPress platform because it is incredibly popular. "How popular, Mark?" you may ask. According to https://techjury.net/blog/percentage-of-wordpress-websites/:

1. More than 30% of the world's websites are in WordPress.
2. More than 75 million websites are in WordPress.
3. 313,050 of the top 1 million websites are in WordPress.

I installed a plugin that lets me log successful and failed logins. Let's walk before we run while reading logs. Read these logs from the bottom. The top entry is therefore the most recent.

Brad Cracker

I am taking control here. Remember, I am the sinister persona.

I intentionally tried logging in with incorrect passwords. I also tried with my VPN client while connected to Stockton, San Jose and Zurich.

ID	Severity	Date	User	IP	Object	Event Type	Message
1002	⚠	02-11-2020 5:33:48.553 AM	Daphne Prancer Author	179.43.139.151	User	Failed Login	
1002	⚠	02-11-2020 5:33:12.043 AM	Daphne Prancer Author	216.151.183.203	User	Failed Login	
1002	⚠	02-11-2020 5:32:45.409 AM	Daphne Prancer Author	173.134.242.42	User	Failed Login	

Figure 29: Intentionally unsuccessful logins from Stockton, San Jose and Zurich.

Seeing that I have Daphne's password, I am logging in as Daphne, creating a new page and deleting another.

ID	Severity	Date	User	IP	Object	Event Type	Message
2012		02-11-2020 5:39:32.907 AM	Daphne Prancer Author	179.43.139.151	Post	Deleted	Moved the post **Test Page** to trash ID: **23** Type: **post** Status: **published** View post in the editor
2001		02-11-2020 5:39:08.031 AM	Daphne Prancer Author	179.43.139.151	Post	Published	Published the post **Home** ID: **25** Type: **post** Status: **published** URL: http://cybersafetynet.biz/home/ View post in the editor
1000		02-11-2020 5:37:45.967 AM	Daphne Prancer Author	179.43.139.151	User	Login	

Figure 30: Successful login lets me create and delete pages

You think that's bad? Remember Mark's "walk before we run" advice. We were walking. Let's run.

What else can a hacker do with a WordPress password?

I already learned Daphne likes the ***2018Prius*** password. I own her. Let me show you how. Daphne is the administrator of the WordPress website at http://cybersafetynet.biz. The site has three other users:

Alex Lifeson (alex@cybersafetynet.biz) has **Subscriber** access.

Edward Van Halen (edward@cybersafetynet.biz) has **Subscriber** access.

Jimmy Page (jimmy@cybersafetynet.biz) has **Administrator** access.

Username	Name	Email	Role
Alex	Alex Lifeson	alex@cybersafetynet.biz	Subscriber
Daphne	Daphne Prancer	daphneprancer@gmail.com	Administrator
Edward	Edward Van Halen	edward@cybersafetynet.biz	Subscriber
Jimmy	Jimmy Page	jimmy@cybersafetynet.biz	Administrator

Figure 31: The website's original permissions

With Daphne's ***2018Prius*** password, I change the site's roles. This helps me cover my tracks and gives the website administrator more work. I change the permissions to the following:

Alex Lifeson (alex@cybersafetynet.biz) has ~~Subscriber~~ **Administrator** access.

Edward Van Halen (edward@cybersafetynet.biz) has ~~Subscriber~~ **Administrator** access.

Jimmy Page (jimmy@cybersafetynet.biz) has ~~Administrator~~ **Subscriber** access.

Except for Daphne's account, the end result reverses the current privileges.

Username	Name	Email	Role
Alex	Alex Lifeson	alex@cybersafetynet.biz	Administrator
Daphne	Daphne Prancer	daphneprancer@gmail.com	Administrator
Edward	Edward Van Halen	edward@cybersafetynet.biz	Administrator
Jimmy	Jimmy Page	jimmy@cybersafetynet.biz	Subscriber

Figure 32: The website's new permissions

I launch my VPN client, connect to a VPN server in Copenhagen, log in as Daphne and change permissions. The log reveals my mischief.

ID	Severity	Date	User	IP	Object	Event Type	Message
4002	!	02-27-2020 4:52:51 AM	Daphne Prancer Administrator, Superadmin	185.245.84.26	User	Modified	Changed the role of the user **Jimmy** New role: **Subscriber** Previous role: **Administrator** First name: **Jimmy** Last name: **Page** User profile page
4002	!	02-27-2020 4:51:07 AM	Daphne Prancer Administrator, Superadmin	185.245.84.26	User	Modified	Changed the role of the user **Edward** New role: **Administrator** Previous role: **Subscriber** First name: **Edward** Last name: **Van Halen** User profile page
4002	!	02-27-2020 4:50:31 AM	Daphne Prancer Administrator, Superadmin	185.245.84.26	User	Modified	Changed the role of the user **Alex** New role: **Administrator** Previous role: **Subscriber** First name: **Alex** Last name: **Lifeson** User profile page
1000	⚠	02-27-2020 4:49:30 AM	Daphne Prancer Administrator, Superadmin	185.245.84.26	User	Login	

ID	Severity	Date	User	IP	Object	Event Type	Message
5006		02-27-2020 5:09:07 AM	Alex Lifeson Administrator, Superadmin	216.151.184.176	Theme	Activated	Theme "**90s Retro**" Install location: **/home1/markg/public_html/cybersafetynet.biz/wp-content/themes/90s-retro**
5005		02-27-2020 5:09:01 AM	Alex Lifeson Administrator, Superadmin	216.151.184.176	Theme	Installed	Theme: "**90s Retro**" Install location: **/home1/markg/public_html/cybersafetynet.biz/wp-content/themes/90s-retro**
2012		02-27-2020 5:07:53 AM	Alex Lifeson Administrator, Superadmin	216.151.184.176	Post	Deleted	Moved the post **A sample home page** to trash ID: **2** Type: **page** Status: **published** View post in the editor
1000		02-27-2020 5:07:19 AM	Alex Lifeson Administrator, Superadmin	216.151.184.176	User	Login	

I now login as Alex. My agenda is to a) delete the home page and b) change the theme to one of the ugliest themes available. I reset my VPN client to Toronto and launched my agenda. Read these logs starting at the bottom.

Forensic investigators geolocate 216.151.184.176 to Toronto. Logged in as Alex, I needed less than two minutes to break your website. How long would it take you to learn it was broken?

Who would tell you? A client, A prospect? A vendor?

When the forensics team investigates this incident, they point fingers at Daphne. When Daphne says she was not the guilty party, they geo locate 185.245.84.26 (page 52) and trace it to Copenhagen, Denmark. Read these logs starting at the bottom.

But wait there is more. I create more mischief. I reset my VPN client to Denver and try logging in as Edward. I enter the wrong password intentionally, to give the forensics team even more to solve.

I try logging in as Edward. The log file merely shows edward@cybersafetynet.biz. Nothing fancy in the log, but it does help preoccupy the forensic investigators. Edward and his failed logins are a decoy. If you find failed logins in any logs, track down the user. Pray that he/she is a legitimate user with an old or saved password that no longer works.

ID	Severity	Date	User	IP	Object	Event Type	Message
1003	⚠	02-27-2020 4:58:10 AM	System	64.145.93.194	System	Failed Login	6 failed login(s) Download the log file.

After you pay a few thousand dollars to restore the original home page and reset all account permissions (and passwords) you get called into a meeting.

The primary questions are:

1. We have hackers in Copenhagen, Denver and Toronto. Where else do we have enemies?
2. How did Alex and Edward gain Administrative privileges?
3. Why did Jimmy lose his?
4. Daphne, this all started with you. How do you explain your actions?
5. Why did this happen and how do we prevent this from happening again?

Get ready for the answers

I used a VPN client to connect to varied cities and access your server. I changed these permissions to throw you off my track. This all started with Daphne's password, which she provided me when she clicked a link she should not have clicked (from page 5) and typed her password at my fake (spoofed) Gmail login page. Good luck remaining employed, Daphne.

If I were super sinister, I would change Daphne's password. Daphne could be you.

Surrender Media (Social Media)

Real social media connections

Mark Anthony

Our generation is the first to utilize social media. We connect with long lost friends, neighbors and our peers. We sign in, review connection requests and accept the requests. We assume the profiles are legitimate. That is not a fair assumption.

Celebrities have a tool to prove they are truly who they say they are. Twitter presents blue check marks to verify celebrity identities.

Figure 33: Verify celebrity social media identities are legitimate

Several people would love to impersonate these celebrities and leverage their reputations. Twitter let these celebrities verify their personas. We can trust these personas. They are legitimate. They have the blue check mark.

There is no authentication tactic to verify regular folk profile information is accurate. When I say, "regular folk," I am talking about those of us who are not celebrities. We send connection requests to each other and trust the profiles are legitimate.

Fake social media connections

Brad Cracker

Let me introduce you to some friends. They may send you connection requests.

1. **Cassandra**. Single mom. Receptionist for a federal government agency's Los Angeles office. Helps establish neighborhood watches throughout Los Angeles County. Tells her kids and neighbors the country will be screwed up until we elect a woman President.
2. **Tom**. Single. Medical student. Works part time at a coffee shop in Palo Alto. Plays computer games in his precious free time. Promises to cure dementia, which has stricken his grandmother. Tells friends the country will be screwed up until we elect Bernie Sanders President and he cancels student loan debt.
3. **Lynne**. Happily married to a professional athlete. Real estate agent in San Francisco. Runs three marathons a year. Promised her mom she would visit all seven continents before turning 50. Laughs and walks away when you try talking politics.

They all appear like decent, honest people. Cassandra wants safe neighborhoods. Tom wants to cure dementia. Lynne wants to travel. You can get connection requests from any or all of them. They are all legitimate. Right?

Cassandra

Single mom. Receptionist for a federal government agency's Los Angeles office. Helps establish neighborhood watches throughout Los Angeles County. Tells her kids and neighbors the country will be screwed up until we elect a woman President.

Accept her connection request. Yes/No?

Tom

Single. Medical student. Works part time at a coffee shop in Palo Alto. Plays computer games in his precious free time. Promises to cure dementia, which has stricken his grandmother. Tells friends the country will be screwed up until we elect Bernie Sanders President and he cancels student loan debt.

Accept his connection request. Yes/No?

Lynne

Happily married to a professional athlete. Real estate agent in San Francisco. Runs three marathons a year. Promised her mom she would visit all seven continents before turning 50. Laughs and walks away when you try talking politics.

Accept her connection request. Yes/No?

Think twice. They're all fake.

I visited https://www.thispersondoesnotexist.com/ and chose three pictures for this book. I wrote the profiles from scratch. https://www.thispersondoesnotexist.com/ uses a generative adversarial network, defined at https://en.wikipedia.org/wiki/Generative_adversarial_network to create pictures. Wikipedia tells us "a GAN trained on photographs can generate new photographs that look at least superficially authentic to human observers, having many realistic characteristics."

Take a deep breath and read that Wikipedia quote again.

> *"A GAN trained on photographs can generate new photographs that look at least superficially authentic to human observers, having many realistic characteristics."*

The pictures are computer-generated. Although computer-generated, they all show imperfections that make them more credible. Cassandra's earrings are not consistent. Tom's teeth are a little yellow (maybe from drinking too much coffee at work). Lynne probably is not a natural blonde. They all have blurry backgrounds.

How much time do you take before accepting connection requests? Facebook and LinkedIn present these in a list. You glance and choose to accept or ignore. Twitter lets people follow you without asking you first (if your profile is public).

Facebook lets you post content and choose if you want to share it with Public (anyone on Facebook) or your Friends. If your Facebook Friends are fake, then who is seeing information you want to share with people who are ***only friends***?

Maybe Facebook is too liberal with the word "Friends"? Are these people really friends or are they connections? Mark has over 3,600 Facebook Friends, but he has met less than 1,000 of them in person. The remainder are merely online connections.

Harvesting information

The more you share online, the more you volunteer to someone who wants to steal your identity. This information includes where you live, where you work, your education, your family, your car, what you do for fun and your travel plans. Some people post pictures of their kids online. Hackers use this information to build profiles and hijack your identity. Social media is a library, for a hacker performing reconnaissance on you, their next target.

Four-letter words

Mark Anthony

This brings us to the two biggest four-letter words in the online world. I am putting these together. Get ready. The first is ***Face*** and the second is ***book***. Put them together and you get Facebook. When I was promoting my third book ***Attract your ideal customer***, I told audiences Facebook had 550 million subscribers. Facebook now has over 2 billion active users.

However, life is not a bed of roses for the Facebook corporation. Disgruntled users accuse Facebook corporation of selling our personal data and in some cases, selling it to parties that interfered in our 2016 federal elections. These claims got the CEO, Mark Zuckerberg, called into the principal's office. I mean, Congress.

Yes, we have learned Facebook sells our information. Information we volunteered to Facebook.

One day, I noticed Facebook presenting me ads for a Michigan State University branded Mastercard. "How effective," I thought. It's as if the advertiser knew I graduated Michigan State University and not one of the California schools. How did they.... ah yes, now I remember.

I told Facebook I graduated from Michigan State University. I did it back when I was creating my Facebook profile in 2009. The more information you provide, the easier it is for Facebook to present people you may want to friend on Facebook. It works. I have friended several classmates from Michigan State University. I lost touch with them, but with the magic of Facebook's algorithms, I now see them and send them friend requests. We thought it was free. We now know better.

Facebook is free?

How much are you paying to use Facebook each month? "Haha Mark, trick question," you may say. "It's free. I am paying nothing." I beg to differ.

You are paying with your personal information. Let me introduce Tanya, one of my fellow MSU alums. I found her on Facebook. I sent a friend request and she accepted within 24 hours. We both told Facebook we graduated Michigan State University. On the UP side, sharing that information helped us connect. On the DOWN side, we shared information Facebook monetizes.

Getting back to the Michigan State University branded Mastercard, the advertisers created the MSU branding and then purchased (or leased) a list of Facebook subscribers who listed Michigan State University as their alma mater. The advertisers also could have asked for graduation dates between 1985 and 2000. I qualify. They know. Tanya and I both volunteered that information.

How come Tanya and I are upset at Facebook for selling our personal information and in turn getting rather specific ads for an MSU-branded Mastercard? The close rate must be higher than for a generic Mastercard. I'm sure the advertisers had a rewarding ROI. We volunteered information that helped them target us.

Some folks are now complaining. They tell Facebook where they went to school, where they live and where they work. That information is sold to advertisers who seek a target audience with those criteria. Some complain. In response, let me ask:

1. How do you expect Facebook Corporation to keep the lights on if they offer free memberships?
2. Where will they get the money?
3. What information do they have that they can monetize?
4. How do you justify your privacy complaints if you volunteer information?
5. How do you protect your personal information while at the same time volunteering that information to help find people, places and activities you may find interesting?

I argue we surrender our privacy. That's why I titled this section "Surrender Media." As soon as we volunteer information to a free service like Facebook, we surrender. As soon as we apply for a car loan, student loan or mortgage, we surrender. The information we surrender (I mean, share), helps us qualify for that loan. It also helps others add us to a group of their potential target market.

Don't criticize Mark Zuckerberg for selling our information. We volunteered it, remember? We use his service for free. Don't call your Congressman and urge him to investigate Facebook. They did not steal. I would argue it is you, who volunteered personal information and realized after the fact that you surrendered (I mean overshared) too much.

When we create that first Facebook account and go through the profile creation wizard, we can hardly see 10 feet ahead of us. We get a smorgasbord of questions, such as:

1. Where and when born?
2. Grade school?
3. Education achieved?
4. High school?
5. College?
6. Marital status?
7. Spouse name?
8. Where you work or have worked?
9. Then we get to the most dangerous ones. Get ready:
   a) Political views?
   b) Religious views?

I wisely answered the dangerous ones. I wrote "Everybody vote for me" and "Everybody worship me." Wise before my time, I suppose.

I challenge you to look at your Facebook profile and see what information you are sharing. Remember Facebook is packaging this and selling it to advertisers. My friend Karl Palachuk says you are the product and he was the first to share that assessment with me. You truly are, especially because you are using Facebook for free.

Look at your profile and see what personal information you surrendered. Ask if you are comfortable with that level of sharing. Also ask how that feeds into the ads you routinely see on Facebook. Remember, Facebook presented me with an ad for a Michigan State University branded Mastercard. If I had not told Facebook I was an MSU alum, they may have presented me with one from a closer school, such as Sacramento State, University of California at Davis or Berkeley.

You can also request that Facebook report to you the information you have shared. Think of this as "You shared this, remember?" Facebook notified us at the start of 2020, when the ***California Consumer Privacy Act*** took effect. I accepted Facebook's offer to download my data and review it. Now that I have, I see what potential clients see when vetting me. Let us all remember, once you put something online, you never know where it will end up.

One of my clients runs 10 beauty salons. He hires teenagers to serve as receptionists and earn minimum wage. The hiring process is no cake walk. The hiring manager receives resumes and then vets candidates online. Yes, you read that right. She Googles the candidate's name and then looks for that candidate online. Facebook is one obvious theater. Others include LinkedIn, Snapchat and Twitter. If a minimum wage receptionist candidate gets vetted online, everybody does.

How Facebook tracks

Facebook tracks the links you click by appending the links. One day, my friend Stephanie Chandler sent me a link via Facebook Messenger. She sent me a link to https://nonfictionauthorsassociation.com/book-editors-recommended-resources. I clicked the link and found https://nonfictionauthorsassociation.com/book-editors-recommended-resources/?fbclid=IwAR3bT5s5HyMYG1JdNh7c2E7YAl_NHSO8ovtXLWJ1XUtvllz_3INPN8lU7qg in the address bar. This link contained Stephanie's original link plus a Facebook tracking code of ***IwAR3bT5s5HyMYG1JdNh7c2E7YAl_NHSO8ovtXLWJ1XUtvllz_3INPN8lU7qg***. Facebook records I clicked that link and will probably find other interesting pages both at https://nonfictionauthorsassociation.com and at related sites.

Facebook acknowledges recording

It is not a secret. We share more information at Facebook than at most other online services. Sometimes we forget how much we share and that what goes online never really leaves online. I asked Facebook to export my personal information back on December 28, 2019. Facebook sent me a thorough response. Here's the response.

"Thanks for contacting us about how to access or download your personal information. You can access your Facebook information using our self-service tools. To get specific types of your Facebook information, such as photos, posts, reactions and comments, visit the Access Your Information tool: https://www.facebook.com/your_information/?ref=cr

You can also download a copy of your Facebook information using the Download Your Information tool: https://www.facebook.com/settings?tab=your_facebook_information

You can download your information in an HTML format that is easy to view, or in a JSON format, which will allow you to transfer your information to another service.

For more information on how to download your information and what's in your downloaded file, please visit the Help Center: https://www.facebook.com/help/212802592074644/?ref=cr

Downloading your information is a password-protected process that only you can initiate. Once you've created a file, it will be available for download for a few days.

Your downloaded file may contain sensitive information. You should keep it secure and take precautions when storing, sending or uploading it to any other services.

To learn more about the categories of your Facebook Information available to you, please visit the Help Center: https://www.facebook.com/help/930396167085762/?ref=cr

Finally, we also encourage you to review our Data Policy, which provides a description of the information we collect and how it is used and shared. https://www.facebook.com/policy.php

If you want to learn more about the categories of information we collect, how we use it, categories of sources, and the types of parties with whom it may have been shared in the last 12 months, you can review our California Privacy Notice: https://www.facebook.com/legal/policy/ccpa

If you have another question or concern, please visit Privacy Basics (https://www.facebook.com/about/basics) or the Help Center (https://www.facebook.com/help) for additional information.

If you have more questions about our California Privacy Notice (https://www.facebook.com/legal/policy/ccpa), please reply to this email.

Thanks,
The Facebook Team"

What Facebook remembers

Facebook staff responded within a few days. To say the data gathered was thorough would be an understatement. Here is what Facebook reported back to me (what I forgot I had posted on Facebook).

> **Mark Anthony Germanos posted in I live in California because....**
>
> Illinois has awful weather in November, December and January. It is worse in February. One morning in February, I decided to wear sunglasses in the morning. Bad idea. The moisture from my eyes froze my eye lashes to my sunglasses.

Figure 34: Among my first Facebook posts. Remembering why I moved from Chicago

Figure 35: From March 3, 2011. What a computer guy does with a phone book

Figure 36: From April 23, 2012. I have not thought about my TV station tour for years

I forgot about these posts. Facebook hasn't.

I am conservative when it comes to sharing personal information that a thief (physical thief or identity thief) would find valuable. Some of my friends are not as conservative. I would label their sharing as sloppiness.

Examples of sloppiness

Sometimes people aren't as street smart as they choose to believe. I am changing my friends' names here.

Ann took a picture of an envelope and posted it on Facebook. This envelope had her name, address, city, state and zip. She also told Facebook she was leaving town for 10 days to visit a friend in Hawaii. Two weeks later, she told Facebook her home was burglarized. I told her she presented valuable information to a potential thief. "Ah yes, I think you're right, Mark," she replied.

Jen posted her address and pictures of her home on Facebook. She also told Facebook she was leaving town to run a retreat. I told her she presented valuable information to a potential thief. She replied, saying that her neighbors agreed to watch her home. "What's wrong with that, Mark? Her neighbors are watching the house, right?" you may ask. She is making her neighbors act as volunteer security guards. Are they contracted to keep watch 24x7? I do not think so.

Ken posted pictures of his kids online. He also posted his address, since he receives work mail at home. He also routinely tells Facebook when he is out of town for training, workshops and other events. A predator can do a little research, find his adorable kids and learn when Ken will be out of town. Nothing has happened yet. Let's hope a predator does not find Ken's kids. Let's hope Ken reduces the amount of information he shares online.

Is Facebook collecting too much information?

"Thanks Mark. I now see Facebook is collecting too much information about us. I am calling my Congressman. That Zuckerberg guy better fess up to what he is doing." I know you are thinking that.

Actually, Facebook CEO Mark Zuckerberg has been called into the principal's office twice. He testified on April 10, 2018 and October 23, 2019. Congress asked if users could protect their privacy. Mark Zuckerberg said they agree to the Terms of Service at https://www.facebook.com/terms.php. The *Terms of Service* page links to the *Data Policy* page at https://www.facebook.com/about/privacy/update. The *Data Policy* states, "We collect the content, communications and other information you provide when you use our Products, including when you sign up for an account, create or share content, and message or communicate with others."

This of course includes my pictures from the TV station tour and the phone book acting as a doorstop. Do not act surprised when Facebook monetizes your data or shares information you thought was private. You shared this content and you use Facebook for free.

Oversharing homework

What have you shared with Facebook? What have you shared online in general? Here is your homework.

1. For Facebook users, visit https://www.facebook.com/settings?tab=your_facebook_information. You may have to login to see this page.
2. Go to the Download Your Information row
3. Click View
4. Download as HTML.
5. Even if you don't use Facebook (and some of my friends have cussed Facebook and closed their accounts) you still have oversharing.
6. Visit Google.com and type your name. Hit (enter) and view the results.
7. Visit Google.com and type your phone number. Hit (enter) and view the results.
8. Visit Google.com and type your full street address. Hit (enter) and view the results.
9. Make notes (below).

Google and Yahoo also track

"But Mark," you may say, "I barely use Facebook. I am safe." Not so fast. You use Google and Yahoo services, right? Google is tracking you. You can also review the data Google is saving and download it, just like we did for Facebook. Google also lets you delete some data.

Gmail tracking

Take a deep breath and visit https://myaccount.google.com/dashboard.

Let's start with the Gmail link. Google indexes Gmail contents and uses that to help determine which ads will be most interesting to us. Let's see how much data Google is collecting.

1. Click the Gmail button.
2. Click GO TO GMAIL.
3. Click All Mail (on the left).
4. Peruse your entire mailbox.

Google reports 4,789 messages in my Gmail account. Although Google reports 4,789 messages, I see only 224 messages in my Inbox, 10 in Trash and 487 in Sent. The rest fall into the categories of Social, Updates and Promotions. I found these categories while proofreading this math. Gmail keeps our messages and uses the contents to help build profiles. Google then uses this profile data to present targeted ads.

You can search within these results. Just go to the "Search mail" box near the top, type a search term and hit (Enter). Here's what I found:

1. ***Expedia*** produced 27 results. Not sure why this happened. I do not use my Gmail account to access Expedia.
2. ***Holly*** (my wife) produced 76 results.
3. ***Nextdoor*** produced infinite results. Gmail stops trying to count.

Page	Result
https://mail.google.com/mail/u/0/#search/Nextdoor	1-50 of about 94
https://mail.google.com/mail/u/0/#search/Nextdoor/p2	51-100 of about 99
https://mail.google.com/mail/u/0/#search/Nextdoor/p3	101-150 of many

I almost forgot I have used Google Drive and FeedBurner. Google recorded my usage.

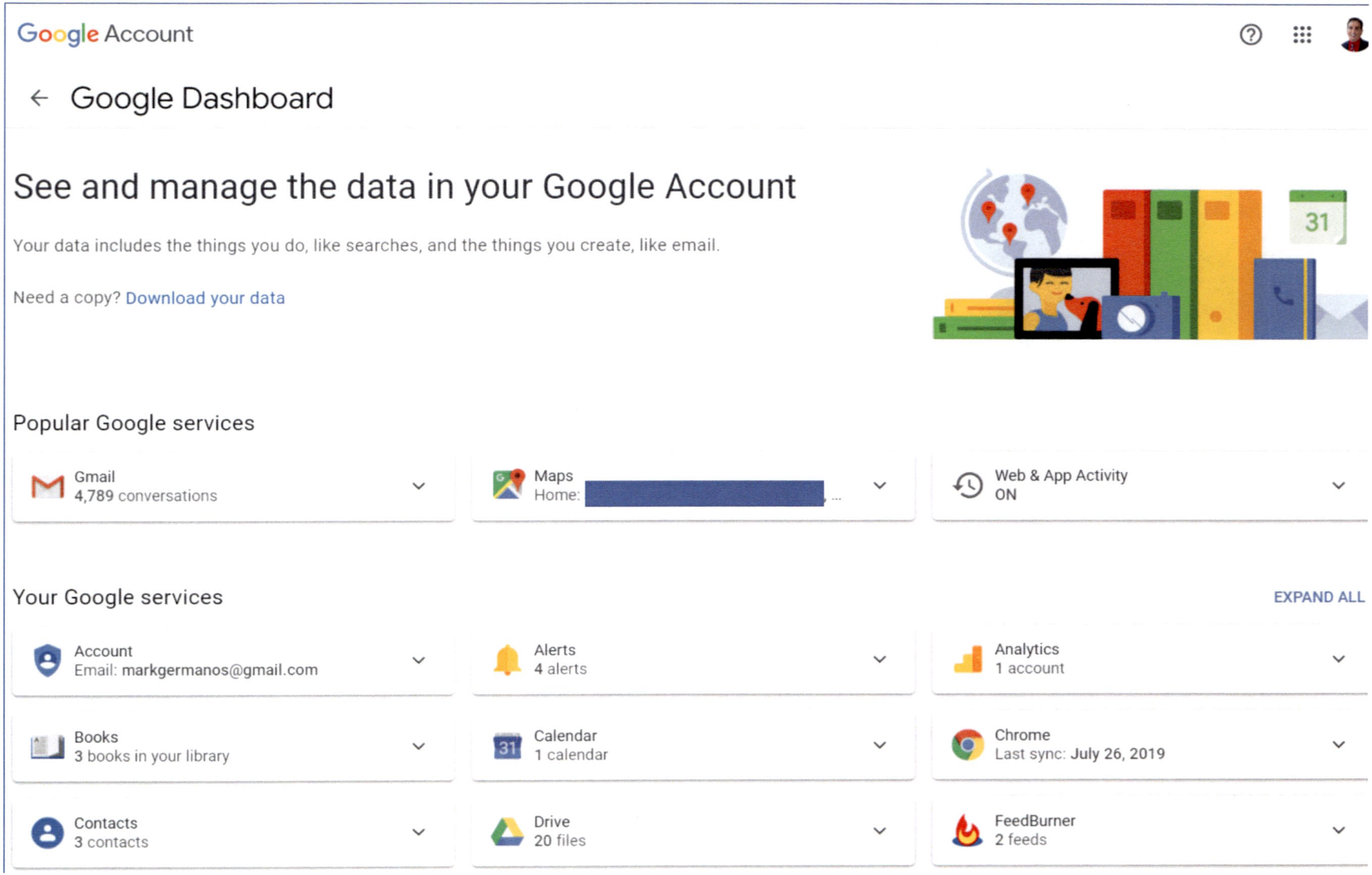

Maps tracking

I redacted my home address. Although intrusive, I understand why this is here. I've asked Google Maps to create directions from my Home.

Web & App Activity tracking

Click Web & App Activity. Google says, "Web & App Activity stores your searches and other things you do on Search, Maps and other Google services, including your location and other associated data." Click Web & App Activity then click the resulting GO TO WEB & APP ACTIVITY.

The results start with the KB4-con conference, and seemingly have no end. This was my most recent Google search. You can drag the scroll thumb all the way to the bottom and then your web browser pushes it up as the web page expands. It's a dangling carrot. I must confess I did not reach the end. I'm writing a book here.

Downloading tracking data

Go back to the Google Dashboard at https://myaccount.google.com/dashboard. Let's just download this data. Click the Download your data link, which takes you to https://takeout.google.com. Scroll through this list of services Google thinks you use. Google checks all by default. At the bottom, click the Next step button.

I am choosing to export this data once, save the data as a .ZIP file and span my data across multiple .ZIP files when the files are larger than 2 GB. Click the Create export button.

Google reports "This process can take a long time (possibly hours or days) to complete. You'll receive an email when your export is done." Google completed my archive within 30 minutes.

Deleting tracking data

Perhaps you feel as I did, out of control. Google does not need to track my web and app data. Go to Google My Activity at https://myactivity.google.com/myactivity?restrict=waa and click "Delete activity by."

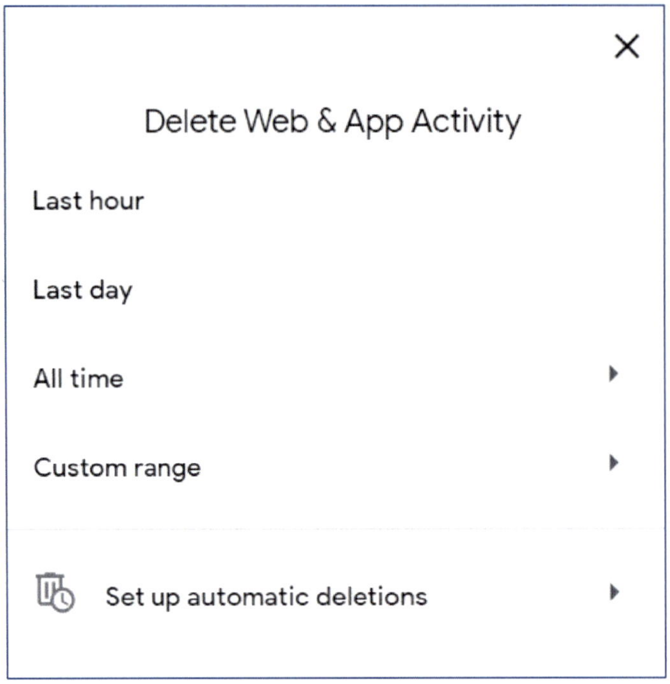

Figure 37: Google lets you delete your web and app activity

I am choosing the last option: Set up automatic deletions.

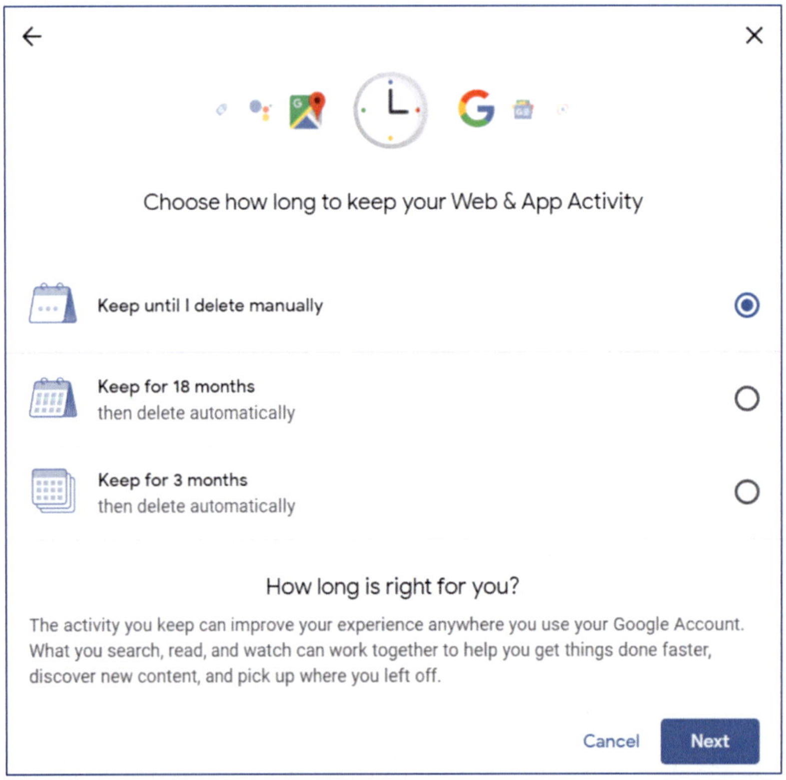

Figure 38: Manually or automatically delete web and app activity. I chose 3 months

Google confirms you always want to delete data that is older than 3 months and you want to trigger this now.

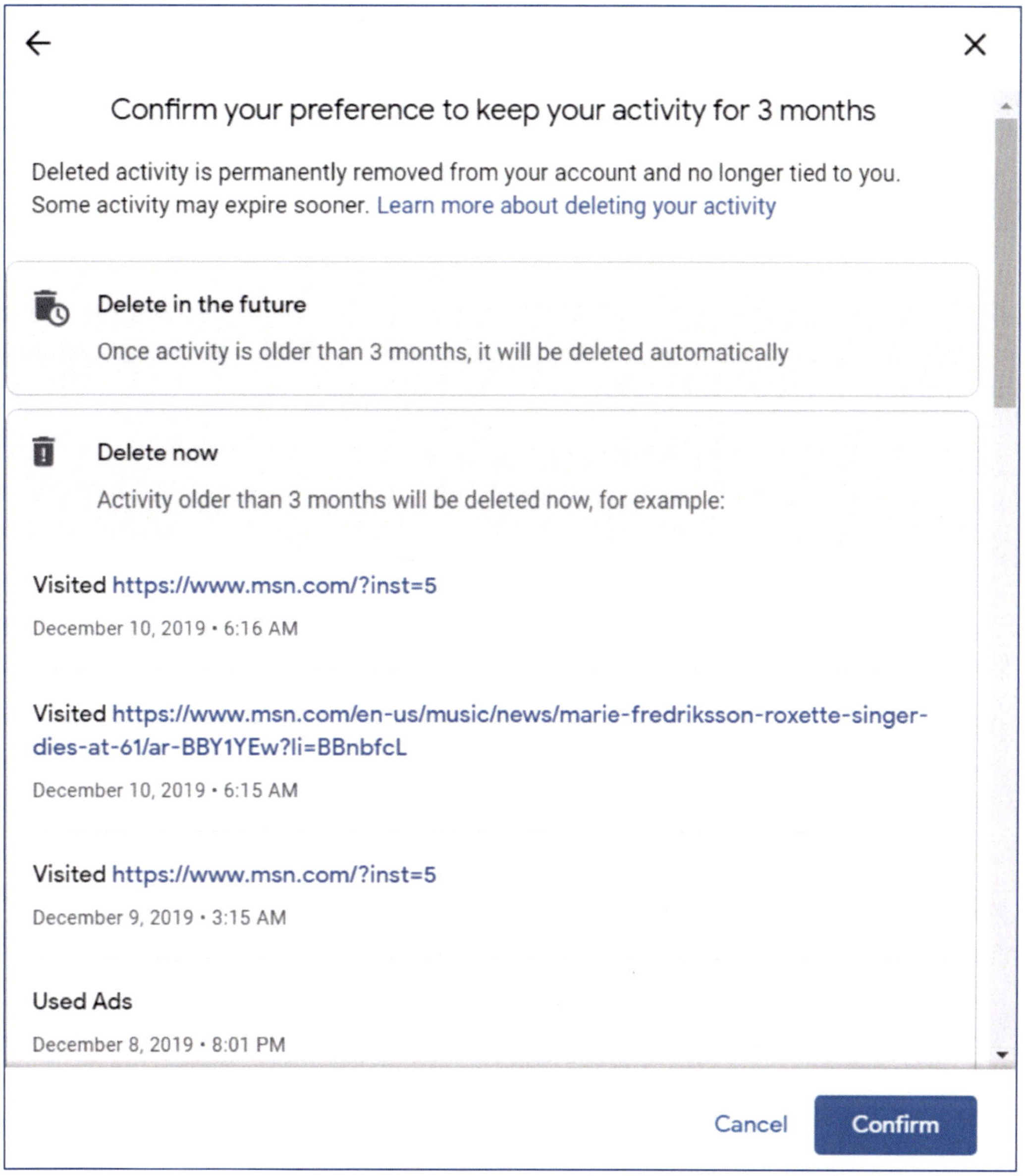

Figure 39: Restrict how much data Google keeps

Gmail monetizes your personal information

For example, https://policies.google.com/terms?hl=en says "When you upload, submit, store, send or receive content to or through our Services, you give Google (and those we work with) a worldwide license to use, host, store, reproduce, modify, create derivative works (such as those resulting from translations, adaptations or other changes we make so that your content works better with our Services), communicate, publish, publicly perform, publicly display and distribute such content. The rights you grant in this license are for the limited purpose of operating, promoting, and improving our Services, and to develop new ones. This license continues even if you stop using our Services..."

Use email that is not free. You get a different privacy policy. I have a Gmail account, but nothing confidential and no ePHI (electronic protected health information) ever transmits through that Gmail account.

Yahoo monetizes your personal information

"But I use a Yahoo account," you may say. Yahoo, as part of Oath, along with sister companies Verizon and America Online, says at https://policies.oath.com/us/en/oath/privacy/index.html "Oath analyzes and stores all communications content, including email content from incoming and outgoing mail. This allows us to deliver, personalize and develop relevant features, content, advertising and Services... We also may use the information we have about you for the following purposes:

1. Provide, maintain, improve, and develop relevant features, content, and Services.
2. Analyze your content and other information (including emails, instant messages, posts photos, attachments, and other communications). You can review and control certain types of information tied to your Oath account by using Privacy Controls.
3. Fulfill your requests and when authorized by you.
4. Help advertisers and publishers connect to offer relevant advertising in their apps and websites.
5. Match and serve targeted advertising (across devices and both on and off of our Services) and provide targeted advertising based on your device activity, inferred interests and location information."

They said, "match and serve targeted advertising..." Suppose you play tennis often. Yahoo can sell that information to advertisers, who in turn send you ads and SPAM for more tennis equipment.

You agreed to it

"OMG Mark, when did I let these people record all this information on me? It happened when you started using their services.

Google homework

Review the information Google is collecting on you.

1. Visit https://myaccount.google.com/dashboard.
2. Review the services in "Popular Google services."
3. When done, go to Google Takeout at https://takeout.google.com/ and export all data as a .ZIP file.
4. Take a deep breath and read what Google has collected on you and your web surfing habits.
5. Do ***not*** call your Congressman. Google is documenting what you did.

Credit card numbers online

Brad Cracker

Stealing passwords helps you steal someone's identity. Stealing credit card numbers helps you buy things while someone else pays. A hacker would enjoy a long list of credit card numbers. I'm sure you see the appeal. Some hackers do not label stealing and selling credit card numbers a crime.

Credit card numbers fall into two categories. Empty and Live.

Empty credit card numbers help you enroll for free services. The credit card numbers don't work for purchasing anything, but they do help you enroll for a free service. The folks at https://techywhale.com/empty-credit-card-numbers/ introduce this concept with "When you try to claim your free trial period on any website, most sites will ask you to submit your credit card details to proceed. But what if you don't own a credit card or are simply paranoid about submitting your credit card details. In that case, a fake working credit card number does the trick. Also known as empty credit card numbers, they are generated randomly by special online generators."

Live credit card numbers work. You can buy almost anything with a valid VISA or Mastercard number.[v]

Type	Number	CVV	Expiration	Name
VISA	4929573268781875	423	03/2022	Jesse Navarro
VISA	4532750306722348	475	04/2022	Patricia Ellis
VISA	4485595500272153	256	12/2022	Edgar Austin
VISA	4539011839324067	343	01/2023	Joshua Kyle
VISA	4147400134874674	417	06/2023	Mark Germanos
Mastercard	5180367408912784	072	10/2023	June Morse
Mastercard	5439433765809218	525	06/2023	Mary Hart
Mastercard	5501957644233456	745	05/2024	Sandra K. Gilbert
Mastercard	5145634085487644	876	10/2023	Ana Hazen
Mastercard	5152583485776041	654	07/2022	Joseph Lewis

I am stopping at 10. I think you get the picture. Empty credit card numbers only help you enroll for online services and provide a valid response to get you over the "provide a credit card number here" challenge. These do not work for making actual purchases. Live credit card numbers work.

You may have noticed one for Mark. This is one he left in a restaurant. After discovering it was lost, he called the charge card issuer, reported it lost and canceled that account. They sent another VISA card the next day.

Yes, you can buy ***Live*** credit card numbers on the dark web. We have several tactics. Physically, we pick pockets, snatch purses or mug our victims. Electronically, we install keystroke loggers or entice you to visit a fake website and type in your charge card number.

A manager at one of Mark's clients clicked a link in an email one day. I'm sure you know where this is going. He purchased $1100 in gift cards and requested the vendor send the gift cards directly to his clients. He waited. He waited. He waited. There were no gift cards. There ***was*** an $1100 charge on the corporate VISA account.

I'm sure you're asking, "What about the security awareness training Mark advocates and his ***keeping security top-of-mind*** mantra?" Sometimes people don't pay attention. Using a computer is like driving a car. You have to pay attention all the time. Look what happens when you don't.

Low-tech hacking

Not all crime is high-tech. Let me introduce you to a low-tech tactic to learn about someone. We call this reconnaissance, which in my world means gathering information about a target. Sloppiness helps make dumpster diving worthwhile. Dumpster diving helps make reconnaissance worthwhile.

Dumpster Diving

What came to mind when you read "dumpster diving"? Was it a poorly dressed man sorting through garbage and looking for documents containing personal information? That is exactly what dumpster diving is.

Junk mail contains valuable information I can use to build a profile of you. We call this PII, or Personally Identifiable Information. Look at what papers you discard every week. This would include the newspaper-like advertising, political fliers, pre-approved credit cards and banks offering pre-printed checks. A dumpster diver can steal these preprinted checks and start buying up the town, on your dime. Dennis Miller calls pre-approved credit card offers "multicolor invitations to identity theft."

Mark Anthony

This also includes, I am sad to report, papers with passwords written on them. I have stopped counting how often I see passwords written on Post-It notes and other papers.

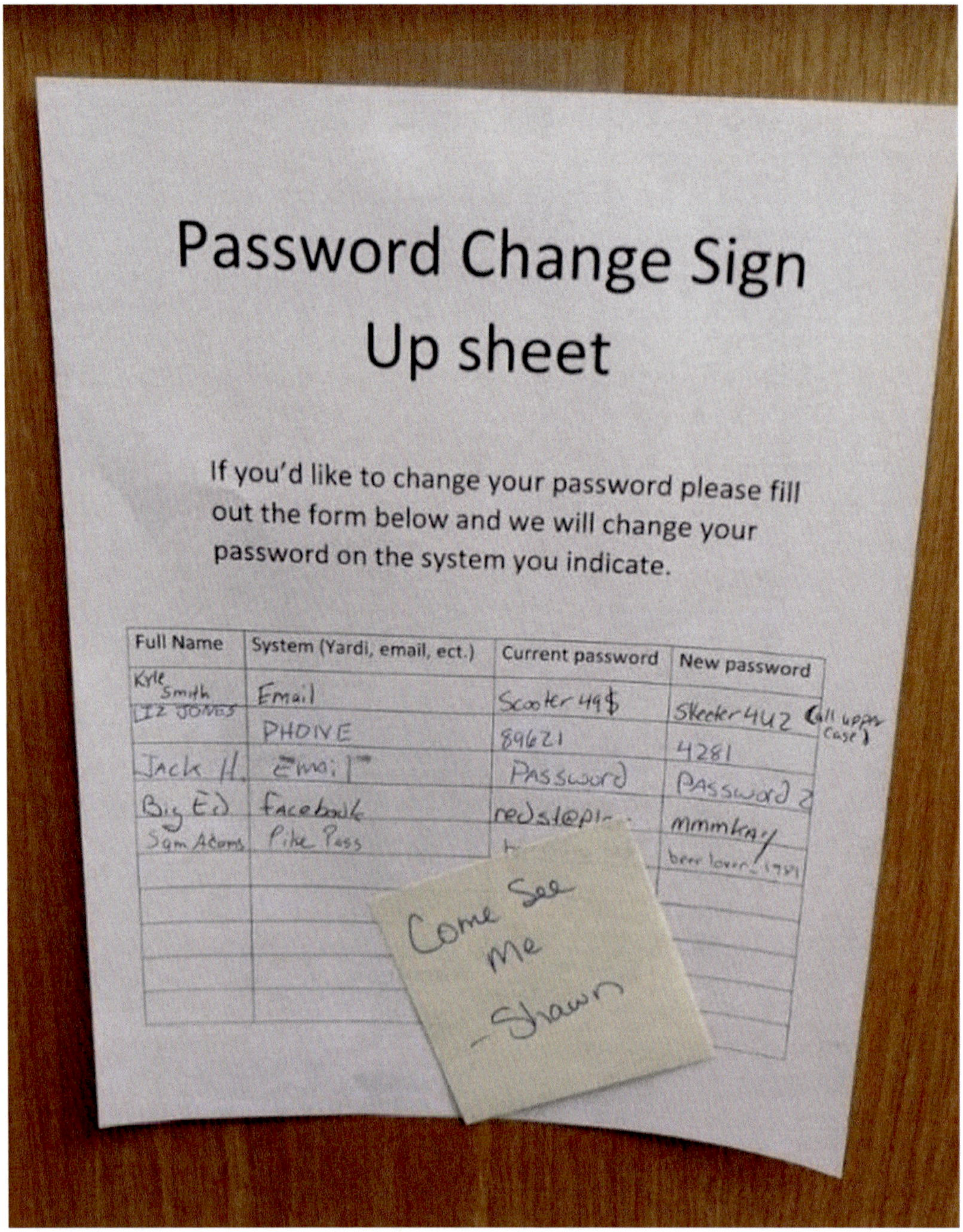

Figure 40: This should never have happened (I found this picture on LinkedIn)

"But Mark, what do I do?" you may ask. You buy a cross-cut shredder and you shred these documents. Any paper with a password written on it should go straight to the cross-cut shredder. With these papers, pre-approved credit card offers and your pre-printed checks in slivers ¼" wide x 1" long, the dumpster diver has a near mission impossible determining what was in the garbage.

I'm hoping you noticed I wrote "cross-cut shredder" and not merely "shredder." A simple (cheap) shredder will cut your paper vertically and leave it nearly intact. This is like looking through mini blinds while watching the neighbors. The brain can still piece together valuable information. A cross-cut shredder makes this task much more difficult.

Figure 41: Too much work to reassemble pages with a crosscut shredder

Storing papers with personal information

Some papers with PII are valuable. Keep them somewhere safe. Some folks have safes in their homes. Some rent safe deposit boxes at the local bank. Some corporations, like Coca Cola, keep secrets in a vault. Any document with your PII should be destroyed or secured. When I say secured, I mean, all the time.

Figure 42: The floor is now open for comments

Junk mail homework

Here is your new homework assignment. Save every piece of junk mail for a month. Document the date received, the sender and what information it contains. You will probably need more than one page. Shred it all at the end of the month.

Junk Mail Collected During ____________________, ________		
Date	Sender	My Personal Information

How to protect yourself

Let's transition from ***how hacks happen*** to ***how to protect yourself***. Some topics here are straightforward while others typically draw resistance from end users.

Convenience vs. security – your comfort level

Remember when I first introduced the spectrum with convenience on one end and security on the other?

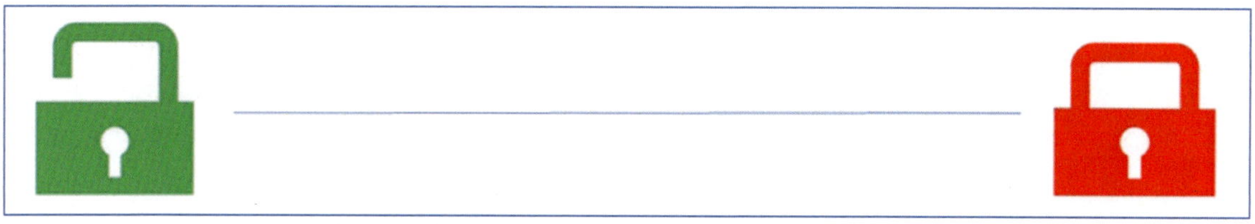

Figure 43: We all live on a spectrum, with 100% convenience on one end and 100% security on the other

Where you reside determines your comfort level with my recommendations. It also determines your resistance. Take a deep breath and continue reading.

Don't share passwords online

Pretty simple advice, wouldn't you say? Even more obvious, I would propose this heightened mandate:

1. Do not write passwords on Post-It notes.
2. If you do write passwords on a Post-It notes, make sure you do not work for an agency that protects our country.
3. If you do write passwords on Post-It notes and you work for an agency that protects our country, do not let somebody take a picture and post that picture online.

I think you know where this is going. On January 13, 2018, Hawaiians' phones buzzed because the government sent an inbound missile alert. Newsweek reported at https://www.newsweek.com/fired-hawaii-worker-who-sent-false-missile-alert-had-mistaken-drills-real-life-795976 "On January 13, the Hawaii Emergency Management Agency erroneously issued alerts to cell phones and broadcast stations across the state warning thousands of people that they were about to be struck by a nuclear attack.

After causing pandemonium that saw Hawaiians scrambling for safety and preparing for imminent death, the agency took nearly 40 minutes to retract the false warning, which came at a time of heightened fears over the nuclear threat from North Korea."

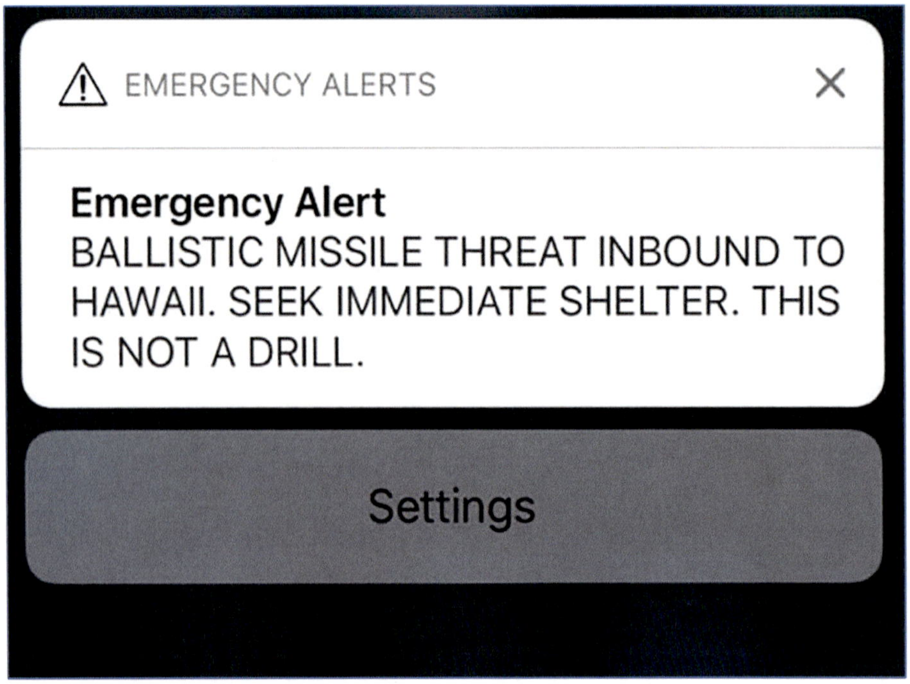

Figure 44: World War III is starting. Kiss your loved-ones good-bye. January 13, 2018

After authorities learned this was a false alarm, forensic investigators asked, “What security measures are the alert staff using?” They found pictures online of a Hawaii Emergency Management Agency staffer with a computer behind him. On the computer monitor was...you guessed it, a Post-It note with a password to Hawaii’s early warning inbound missile alert system.

Figure 45: The early warning defense system at Hawaii Emergency Management Agency apparently has a password of Warningpoint2

This could have gone under the passwords section, but I put it here under how to protect yourself because I found this picture on Twitter.

Least privilege to data

Least privilege means granting employees access to minimal resources until they prove they need more access. Let's look at three departments within your company, and the data members in these groups can access.

Group	Privileges
Executives	Standard info about the office and firm. Product documentation and strategies. Personnel records, including compensation and social security numbers. Confidential information to help the firm compete. Documentation RE: potential mergers and acquisitions.
Human Resources	Standard info about the office and firm. Product documentation and strategies. Personnel records, including compensation and social security numbers.
Sales and Marketing	Standard info about the office and firm. Product documentation and strategies.

A new salesperson comes on board. What information does she need? "Put her in the Sales and Marketing group, Mark," I hear you say. Yes. That makes sense. However, I've stopped counting how often I inherit a network where people are granted access to all data or Everyone has access to all data. "Everyone" is literally a Windows built-in group.

Audit your computers. Initially grant access based on least privilege then assign more privileges for more sensitive groups. Here's how:

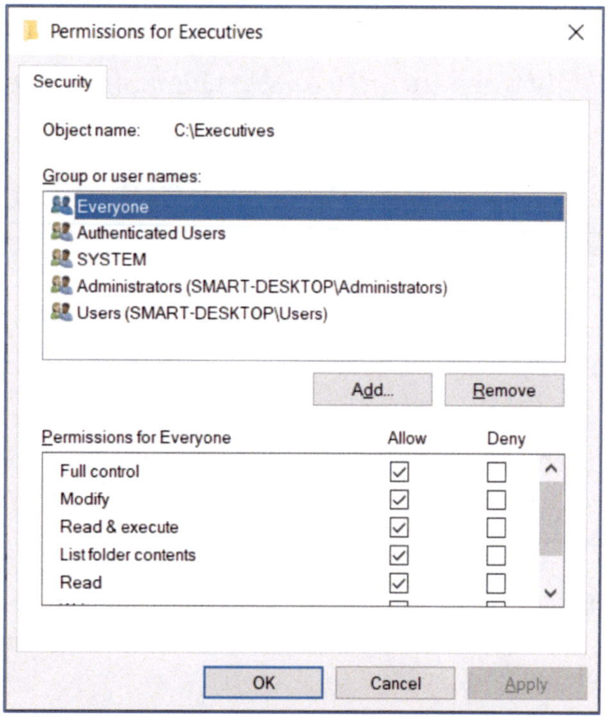

Figure 46: Who can see Executives' data? Everyone

1. Determine which folders have necessary data.
2. Determine which groups, or classification of employees, need access to that data.
3. Populate those groups.

Let's suppose you hire a new salesperson Kim. You'd place her in the Sales and Marketing group. She is superb. You later learn Kim took night classes in Human Resources Administration. She asks for split responsibilities. Part time Sales and Marketing and part time Human Resources. You add her to the Human Resources group. A year later, you promote Kim to Vice President of Human Resources. You place her in the Executives group. As Kim's responsibilities grow, Kim's privileges grow. Make sure your people have ***the least privileges to do their jobs***. Everybody does not need to see what the Human Resources group sees (compensation and social security numbers).

Least privilege to the system

While you're at it, determine who has permissions to change system settings. When you pull a new computer out of the box, plug in the cables, power it up and run the Windows 10 Professional startup wizard, you create an account that is in the Administrators group and does ***not*** have to have a password. I've seen people go through this process and start web surfing.

"The Administrators group?" you may say. Yes. User accounts with administrative privileges have authority to change any system settings. This includes installing and uninstalling software. You're better off (and more secure) creating a standard account for a typical work product, managing email and web surfing while using an administrative account only when ***intentionally*** changing system settings.

I created two accounts.

Account name	Notes
Joe Smith	Standard privileges for email, web surfing and other routine work product.
Joe-Admin	Administrative privileges for installing software, uninstalling software or changing system settings. Share the password only after receiving the client's direction to do so.

This helps secure workstations. Sometimes we call this ***locking down*** or ***hardening*** workstations. Here's why we allocate least privilege.

"Mark, you're such a hard ass. I need to do my job and you are locking down my workstation." If I had $1 for every time a user complained about me locking down their workstation, I would live in California.

An application inherits the current user account privileges. If the user is logged in with an account that has administrative privileges, she clicks a link and automatically installs whatever application is the payload of that link. If the user is logged in with a standard account, she clicks a link and sees a User Access Control prompt. This gives her the chance to ask, “Do I really want to install this?”

Kim goes to work early. She checks her email. She sees a link to a website promising a free pizza before 12 noon if she clicks a link. Kim has a new computer and her account has the default administrative privileges. “Hmm, I am running a staff meeting today and have not ordered food yet. Let’s do this,” she utters. She clicks the link. She sees her screen flicker. She minimizes her web browser and finds her desktop wallpaper is now pornography. Kim panics. You now have a hostile workplace.

Two minutes later, Kim and other users report they cannot get to files on the office server. When they try, they get a message that all files have been encrypted and a ransom, payable in Bitcoin, is necessary to decrypt them (make them visible again).

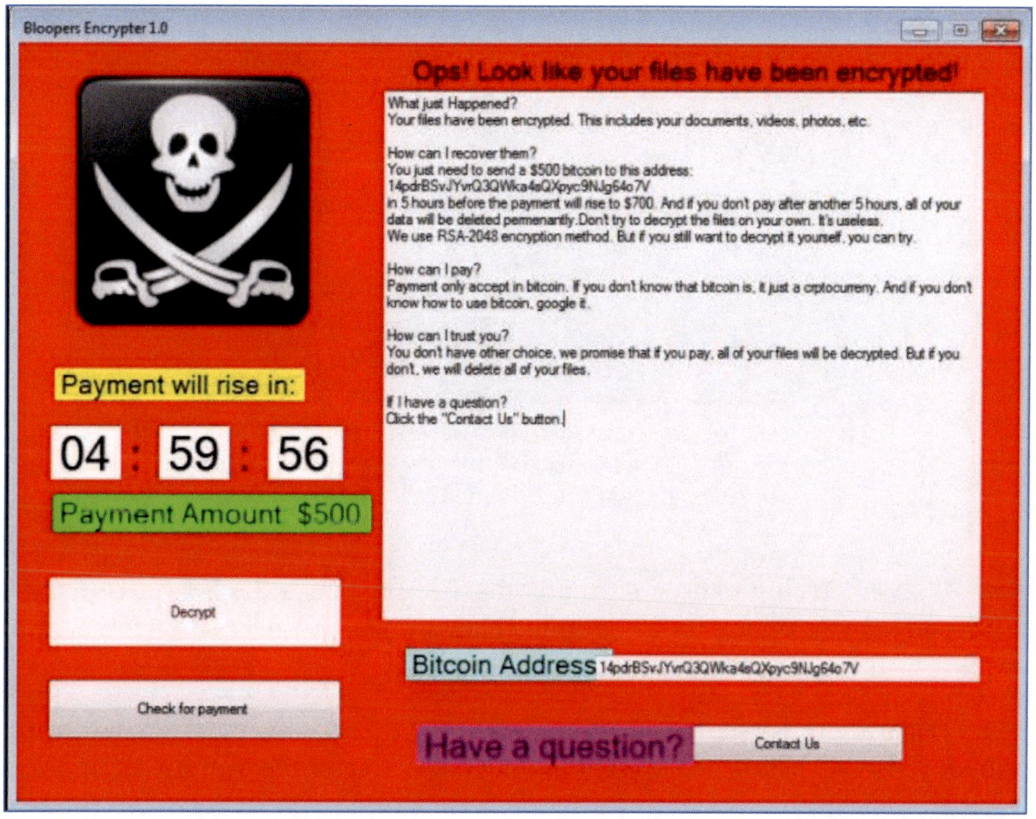

Figure 47: Ransomware installs automatically when you sign in with administrative privileges

You ask everyone if they clicked any suspicious links. Kim fesses up that she clicked a link for free pizza. That happened a few minutes before others reported the ransom demand.

Fearmongering? I do ***not*** think so. A client reported this happened at his corporate headquarters three days ago.

Megan works remotely. She checks her email and sees the same email Kim read. Megan also likes pizza, especially if it is free. She clicks the link. Up comes a Windows User Account Control prompt.

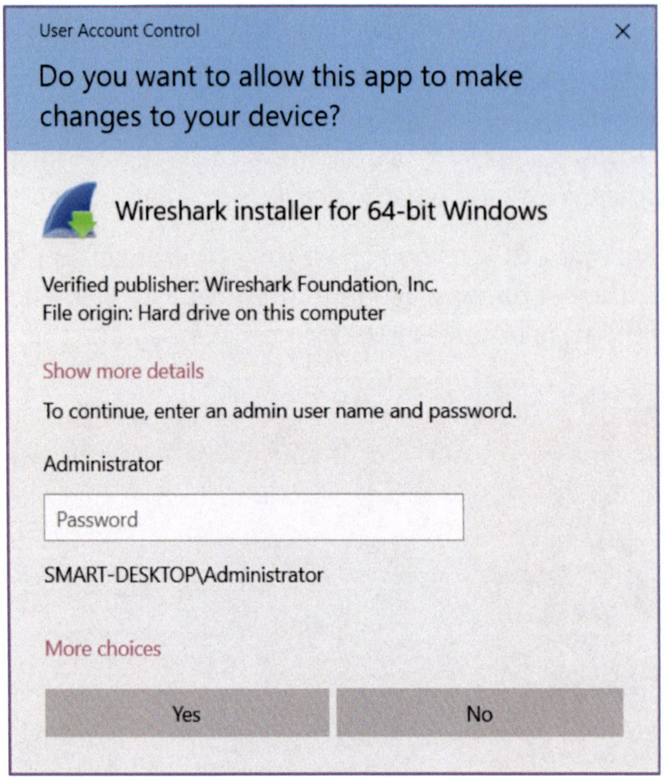

Figure 48: You need an administrative password or administrative privileges to make system changes. This is a good thing

"What the hell is this trying to do?" she screams. Megan clicks the No button and deletes the email. Good. That's what should happen. That's one simple way to protect yourself, your company and your data.

I have users resisting this least privilege policy. They do not want me hardening or locking down their workstations. "But Mark, we need to change system settings and can't deal with that prompt every time." You, as the boss, need to lay down the law. This technology decision is really a managerial decision.

Expiring passwords

Microsoft Windows Server 2016 has a default password change policy that expires passwords every 42 days. Users must change passwords every 42 days, or they lose access to networked resources. I usually set password expiration to 30 days.

You probably do not know when someone is trying to guess your password. Back in the ***What the target's Windows logs report*** section, I showed that a hacker was trying to access a computer.

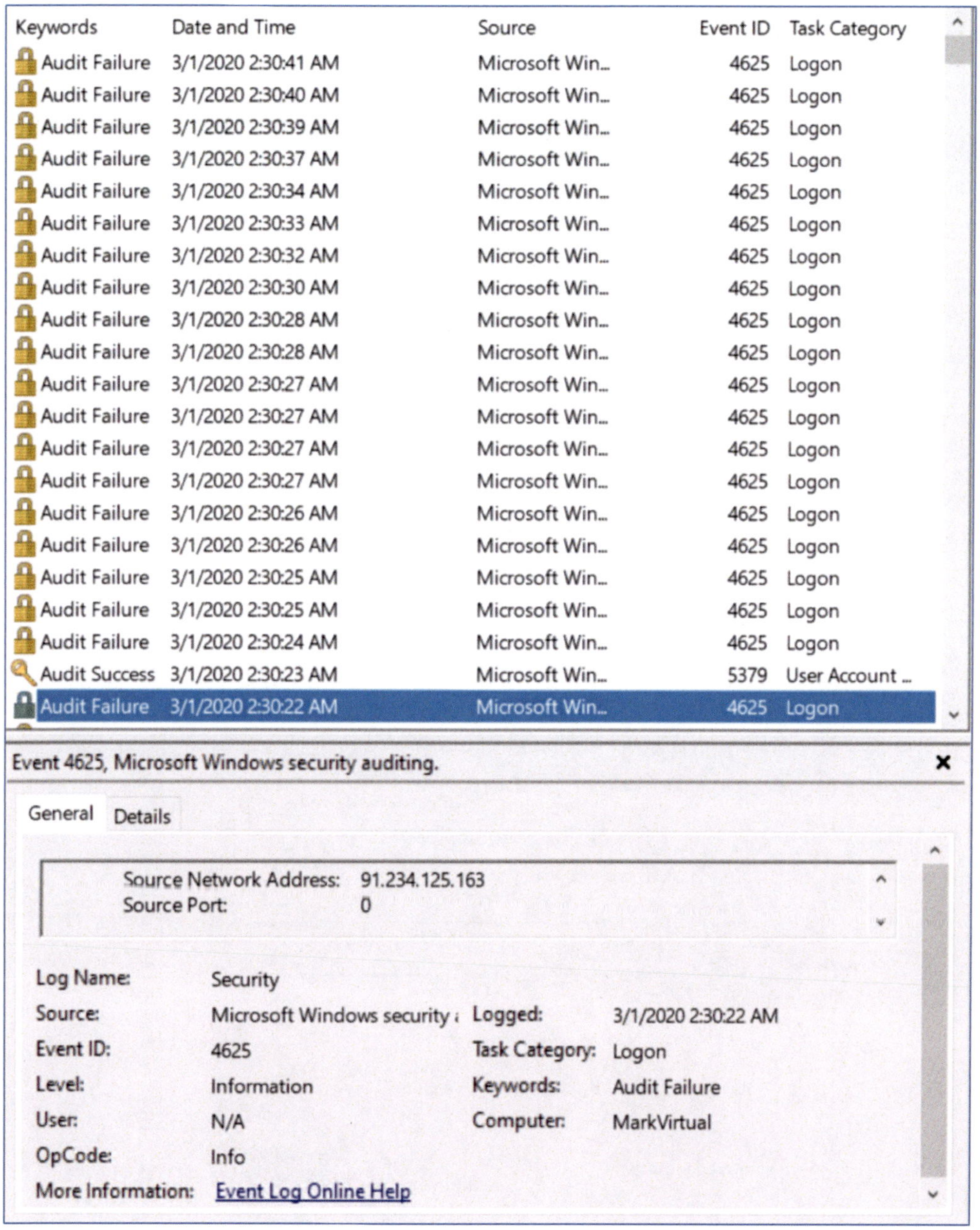

Figure 49: The hacker will eventually stumble across a password that works

He will eventually stumble across a password that works. He is hacking at the rate of 151,200 attempts per day. If you never change passwords, his chances of guessing yours are better than if you force password changes every so often. I set 30-day expiration policies. Microsoft's default is 42 days.

Like the least privilege policy, I have users resisting this password expiration policy. "Every 30 days, I am locked out," they say. "Well then, create a recurring task in Outlook to change your password. Set this to recur every 25 days," I reply. They mumble and look away. Once again, I report, "You, as the boss, need to lay down the law. This technology decision is really a managerial decision."

Centralized virus protection

The need for virus protection is not news. Virus protection is mandatory. Windows includes a free product called Defender. That is not sufficient. "Why not, Mark?" I can hear you complain.

You must prove virus protection works and you are virus free. If any viral activity occurs, you need a notification of a) on which computer and b) what happened. Windows' free Defender does not do this. I resell a product called Webroot. It is not the only centralized protection out there, but it ***does*** meet my criteria. Webroot sends me email when the Webroot agent on any client computer blocks viruses.

Here's another reason you cannot rely on Defender. Remember back in the ***This hack happens every day*** section when I showed you my spoofed Gmail login page?

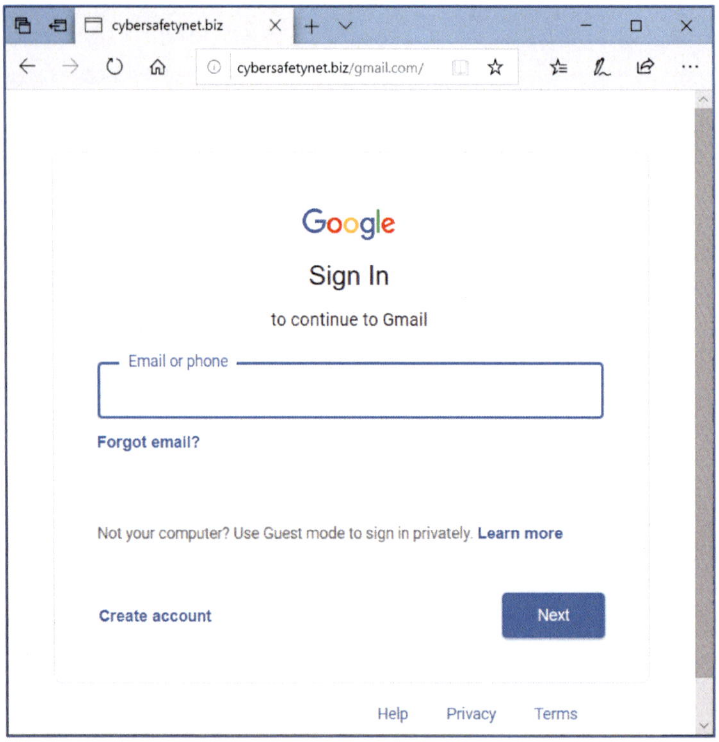

Figure 50: Would your virus protection block this web page? Webroot did. Defender did not

I had to disable Webroot and take screen captures while Defender was protecting (or not protecting) the computer. Nuf said.

Virus protection homework

Is your virus protection active and current? Here is your last homework assignment.

Trait	Notes
Product Name	
License Number	
License Expiration	
Frequency of Program Updates	
Frequency of Signature Updates (lists of viruses)	
Last Scan	
Scheduled Scans	
Last Time Caught or Quarantined a Virus	
Action to Take After Catching a Virus	
Which Computer(s) Monitored	

Are we done yet?

Pretty close.

Being a hacker may or may not be a bad thing. We saw how Mark Anthony is a good guy, a white hat hacker. He wants to protect you. We also saw the alternate persona, Brad Cracker. Brad is a bad guy who wants to exploit you. Brad thinks what he does is not a crime. Hacking is not considered a crime in some countries, provided the government is not a victim.

Hacks happen every day. We met Daphne. Let's review Daphne's blunders. Daphne clicked a link in a phishing email. Daphne provided her ***2018Prius*** password on a fake Gmail login page. Daphne uses that password at several websites. Someone hacked Daphne's work website and set her up to take the blame. Daphne could be you.

Websites challenge you to prove you are who you claim to be. That's why they require passwords. You accumulate passwords and find a password management tool becomes necessary. Whichever tool you choose, just remember something is better than nothing.

You may be great at securing your passwords while your business partners aren't. You can check online to determine if your business partners have reported breaches. If they have, you need to change your passwords. This is the primary reason why we do not reuse passwords across several websites.

You can establish Multi Factor Authentication to provide an extra layer of security. Websites can challenge you on what you know, what you are and what you have. Make sure you establish at least two of these three challenges. **

Black hat hackers thrive because they hide their tracks. We say how a hacker can connect to another city and launch hack attacks from these remote locations. Forensic investigators must sort through misinformation to get to the good information that would help them find and stop a hacker.

We also saw how people surrender personal information online. They do so partly because they do not understand the ramifications of surrendering (oops, I mean...sharing) personal information. Big names such as Facebook, Google and Yahoo monetize that for their benefit. You are the product Facebook, Google and Yahoo sell to advertisers.

You must decide where you and your company reside on the Convenience vs. Security spectrum. Wherever you decide you reside, people will challenge your integrity. People will ask you for administrative passwords so they can "get their work done." Do ***not*** sacrifice security for convenience.

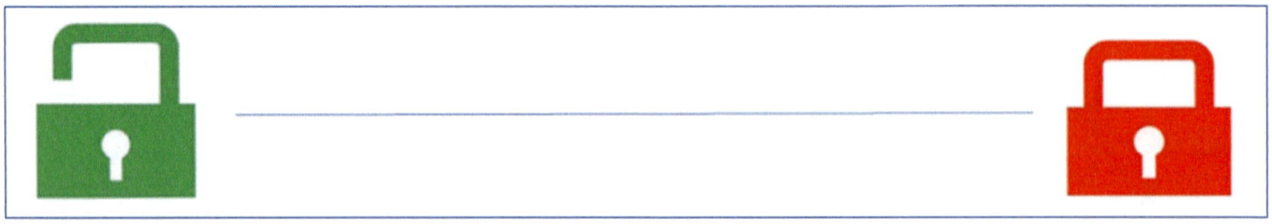

*Figure 51: We all live on a spectrum with 100% convenience on one end and 100% security on the other. Yes, this **IS** the third time I am presenting this graphic*

Your security is as strong as its weakest link, your people. That's why you need security awareness training and you need to keep security top-of-mind. Using a computer is like driving a car. You have to pay attention all the time. Look what happens when you don't.

My primary purpose is to ***keep you safe online***. Just remember: Brad Cracker does not care about you. He wants to steal what you have and sell it. Mark Anthony wants to protect you. I created both personas to show the extremes.

I know your time is valuable. I know you have other things you could have been doing, but you chose to learn how hacks happen and how you can protect yourself. Stay safe out there.

---

[i] A password list from https://pastebin.com/gVs0cbXW The convention is emailaddress: password.

cloudsquall88@gmail.com: squallcloud
eryuga@gmail.com: ryuasorrey9
chase.scully123456@gmail.com: 321Chase
schneeberger23@gmail.com: 74850915a
tokataa98@ABV.bg: zina11
atrwtos93@gmail.com: mhtsiou13
sutirtha1234@gmail.com: rubai1234
hjalmgren__@hotmail.com: w47owh6n
mettalboyX@gmail.com: 53845384
nathan96jones@gmail.com: Maxandpaddy12
keieon.main@gmail.com: niceday1
cejaramillof@gmail.com: c9874123
dilaksantharmalingam@gmail.com: dilaksan00
fallinginthais@gmail.com: tata159753
colinapelc@gmail.com: sevenmile101
Natanin9@gmail.com: GuThRiE98
jaredeyork@gmail.com: abc123cBa
davidchangx1@gmail.com: davidchang
winski.wayne@gmail.com: R00tbeer
creatures213@gmail.com: chronicles1
danyel.kvarnstrom@gmail.com: del3te123
ruifprocha@gmail.com: Rocha2015
bradyskene@gmail.com: cocojimmy
bilalxd@gmail.com: Fanan1220ali
natemcole98@gmail.com: nahtan99
jakeenderwick321@gmail.com: Jake1998
tehextralarge@gmail.com: M1sterman
bennywijayaa7@gmail.com: sakura02
paulius.sigliukas@gmail.com: 4571all34m
viledk@gmail.com: Colonel123
htet.maung1999@gmail.com: tokitoki89
perczok@gmail.com: czubek333
Chriistofffer95@gmail.com: Christoffer95
ruqineko@gmail.com: fallen789
amedeo108@gmail.com: cazziemazzi92
michaelpedersen88@gmail.com: Helmut86
nybnator@gmail.com: signal123
cenaspa3@gmail.com: Casioa168
blythrw@gmail.com: goldie22
ghostaurus18@gmail.com: f25c9a02
brx.871@gmail.com: Juiceman1
galaktikosvaldovas@gmail.com: Lasabliux012
kmekss94@gmail.com: dark3li7e
anton.hakansson17@gmail.com: tegelsten666
cminyovsky@gmail.com: 54565153
dodo.gustafson@gmail.com: omglolnoob231
doug8083@gmail.com: baseball93
horcicko.michal@gmail.com: cucamceciky

mrcow-ohsj@hotmail.com: hahasex911
fjlapostol@gmail.com: planetx69
flexe.sabidong@gmail.com: jerome021991
raivszeltins@gmail.com: raivis96
fredhellamaa@hotmail.com: Harlytuo94
bridgeskody01@Yahoo.com: ghost123
carlwilding@gmail.com: iguits83
fraziercelia@yahoo.com: redskin1
monicanathania30@gmail.com: nathania2001
nielsen72@hotmail.com: 110672
melanie.jordan@umb.edu: allison
openet@gmail.com: hh80151143
orbibiker@gmail.com: 1agatka1
saphireness@gmail.com: saphire1
ryliebayless@Yahoo.com: bayless11
rinee_h@ymail.com: sh1nj1nhw4
rslhanna@Yahoo.com: iama3fan
soniaanggono@hotmail.com: ladidada
tassianinski@gmail.com: tassia13
the_nicologic@Yahoo.com: tangamo
laraofkrypton@Yahoo.com: Acheron23
uthsiy@Yahoo.com: putri13
vrodri04@hotmail.com: e3n94hud
yehxxoo@gmail.com: muma0749
taranicole825@Yahoo.com: stratus05
aarontoy01@gmail.com: aarontoy01
becky1711@Yahoo.com: kendra1711
unyiindhi@Yahoo.com: Unyii1909
fnaveda@hotmail.com: fnaveda3
erwin.ant@gmail.com: Gondar001
michi@goldener.ch: MicGol13
kristoff127: kissnanou127
jeanlima08: lima08
XsabrezX: Password2009
Yes, there are more. I am sure you get the message.

tonkataue@gmail.com: Guitar12
awinckler94@gmail.com: pendulum94
v.rusescu@gmail.com: Chishinau
ktfolse09@gmail.com: spyrad0ula
mbergele@gmail.com: jolanta12
pjp.marikit@gmail.com: channelfix|
diegillomk@gmail.com: Jama1099
cicatl@hotmail.com: fuchico
mei.karen2@gmail.com: d056151710
notphinot@gmail.com: myungs00
npolicky@gmail.com: 42854285
paall1@gmail.com: lnp013050
paulhkeng@gmail.com: sfacsfac
skogh75@gmail.com: smilla
roxanah123@gmail.com: poloh123
tataonoda@Yahoo.com: reta123
rwgray3@gmail.com: irie8675
tculpepper@gmail.com: pepper40
stevent_caesar@Yahoo.com: outlander278
tanuwidjajamonica@gmail.com: daniel27
topdown99@hotmail.com: 6rogue9
wsip021056@gmail.com: peggy0925ip
wilyanto.liang@gmail.com: 828280
xxblake14xx@Yahoo.com: nikko1996
tripleb221@hotmail.com: sherlock99
witt3202@gmail.com: chardie
fennywiradinata@Yahoo.com: pink1981
brett.honey@hotmail.com: carlton3
emmachengty@gmail.com: 971218
jasnowflake88@gmail.com: Mischief88
dre.gonzaga@gmail.com: 721273
josereyes1000: s8687974
madsrathleffj@gmail.com: a96569656
tosot666: 971022

[ii] I am retaining the original graphics and formatting here.

[iii] Although the owner granted permission to hack, I changed the destination IP and redacted the destination IP in the logs.

[iv] Research honeypots are run to gather information about the motives and tactics of the black hat community targeting different networks, from: https://en.wikipedia.org/wiki/Honeypot_(computing)

[v] Although live credit card numbers are available online, too, Mark refused to publish them here. He said, "You've got to be kidding me. We're trying to help innocent people here, not wannabee hackers. They can do their due diligence and find stolen credit card numbers on their own. Nuf said."

Made in United States
Orlando, FL
04 November 2026